PROMETHEANS

ALSO BY BURTON RASCOE:

TITANS OF LITERATURE

FROM HOMER TO THE PRESENT

LUCIAN.

PROMETHEANS

ANCIENT AND
MODERN

BY BURTON RASCOE

G·P·PUTNAM'S SONS·1933
NEW YORK AND LONDON

PN451
R22p

TO THE READER

*

THE identity of the genius who conceived the myth of Prometheus is lost in the mystery of remote antiquity; but let us honor his memory and salute his shade with all the deference due him for having put into an allegory one of the sublimest testimonies to the struggles of the human spirit. It was Prometheus, you will recall, who defied the fearful gods and brought to mankind the gift of fire. For having dared to do this Prometheus was punished by a wrathful Zeus who caused him to be chained to a precipice in the Caucasus where an eagle descended daily to eat out his heart. Daily a new heart grew in its place.

The men and the women who have wrought warmth into the bleak terror of man's war against the elements, against his own nature and against the imminence of death, have brought us out of a savagery that is now at least a savagery modified by an appearance of amenity. They have always suffered and their hearts have been

7

torn out repeatedly by the spectacle of the cruelty men can inflict upon one another in their efforts to survive. But their hearts grow back, for further pluckings, because the belief persists that all the difficulties of life may some day be smoothed away.

I am not sure that would be a blessing. But I have never had experience of such a state, nor do I know of any one who has. The Nirvana of complete tranquillity is, I suspect, an ideal for and by those who have no tranquillity whatever; whereas I have observed that those who achieve an outward appearance of the static condition of tranquillity for any length of time get bored with it and sometimes break out in the most unseemly conduct. They not uncommonly resort to clubs, firearms, or meat-axes.

Still, at the same time, one wishes, in these years of the locust, that there could come some stability and that life would not dance before one's eyes like a species of retina trouble. One wishes that young children were not starving and that feeble old men innocently abroad on their routine affairs were not shot down by gunmen. One wishes above all that wars might cease, disease be conquered, and that kindness, generosity and magnanimity might universally prevail.

A conviction is gaining ground that through a complete socialization of the means of production and of the distribution of wealth the human race will come into a blissful condition. And to realize this conviction, murder and rapine are conducted on a grand scale; there are intrigues and fights for power on the part of those who believe they know better than their rival comrades how to bring about this Utopia, and the victors have caused to be exiled, or have had lined up and shot, those who are weaker in the argument. It quite definitely solves the economic problems of any individual to batter his brains out. Possibly if there are enough individual economic problems disposed of in this manner, a happy grace will pervade the globe.

The great imponderable is that energy is at once the great factor in life and its most sinister potential. It is at least relatively true that power begets power and nothing else. Champions of the weak, even, tend to oppress those weaker than themselves once they have succeeded in their championship of the weak. That is the blighting paradox. All great tyrannies have begun in idealism. All reforms carry with them, like a shadow, the threat of evil.

Yet reforms are inevitable because change is constant in human society and ideas are generated by the irksome desire for variety and improvement. Hence the irony and the tears of things. Humor is a solvent for the brine of tears; and in many of those who are articulate the urge and the genius to provoke a chuckle or a smile is as definite and as sublime, as wise and as beautiful as the urge and the genius to purge the mind by evoking pity and terror.

In these pages I have tried to give, as I tried also in *Titans of Literature,* a reflection of this diversity of man's high articulate response to the circumstances of life, and to write of those who, in the art of literature, have, like Prometheus, brought fire and warmth to their fellow men.

It is eminently desirable that all men should be proficient, successful and potent and that all women should be beautiful, desirable, gracious and fecund and that there should be enough money to go around for all this; and that there should be no quarrels between nations or persons; and that you and I could agree upon every possible subject; and that you should never be able to catch me in error or detect in me what you consider an iniquity; and that I should find no fault whatever in you; and that we could dance to an unbelievable age with our heads knocking out the stars, young, wise, affluent and serene. ... But I am wondering if we shouldn't find that a little tedious after three hundred and sixty-five days of it, or less.

I am afraid we should begin to yearn for poverty, lassitude, recriminations, demolition, sculduggery, rapine, scholastic errors, graft, vice, usury, and deformity of person. Perfection is a goal, to which it might be a disillusion to attain. But we strive toward it, anyway, each in his very limited manner.

Meanwhile, I wish to express my thanks to the Oxford University Press for their kindness in permitting me to use copious excerpts from the translation of the works of Lucian made by the brothers, H. W. and F. M. Fowler. The complete translation by Professor Harmon of Princeton University of the extant works of Lucian for the Loeb library has so far reached only the fourth volume, with the text opposite the translation. The four volume translation by the Fowler brothers is excellent, although it excludes the important disputed work, the *Philopatris,* and is euphemistic here and there.

I wish also to thank Mr. Alfred A. Knopf of Alfred A. Knopf, Inc., for permission to use a quotation from *Memoirs of a Polyglot* by William Gerhardi; Mr. Alfred Harcourt of Harcourt, Brace & Co., for permission to quote from *The Savage Pilgrimage* by Catherine Carswell; The Viking Press, for permission to quote from *The Letters of D. H. Lawrence,* edited by Aldous Huxley.

In all other instances I have given, I hope, proper credit for my sources (when they might not be generally known) in the body of my text. I have not dispensed with footnotes as much as I could wish. Perhaps you will forgive me for this when I whisper that, although I frequently find footnotes disconcerting, sometimes I find them the only agreeable reading in a work of scholarship.

BURTON RASCOE

CONTENTS

*

PROMETHEANS

*

SAINT MARK

SAINT MARK

*

THE Apostolic Fathers were wise and inspired and learned in many matters, but they were very short-sighted in one thing: they failed to realize that, although a healthy disagreement of opinion is a salutary way of arriving at the true (or the expedient) in council, it works havoc when this disagreement is expressed in a canon.

When these pious and argumentative fathers of the Christian church established the canon of the New Testament some three hundred and fifty years after the birth of Jesus, the Christ, they included in this canon of their faith—as we know—four distinct biographies of Jesus, the first three of them differing from one another but also differing so much from the Fourth Gospel as to seem to have been written about two quite different men.

This was a much worse thing for them to have done (from a humane, religious or rational point of view) than it would have been for the delegates to the General Convention in Philadelphia in 1787 to have given us four

Federal Constitutions of the United States of America, all bound up together, each reflecting in considerable degree the disharmony of the peculiar casts of mind entertained by members of the assembly.

Confusion and chaos would have been upon us (even before now) if we had four Constitutions, each one held to be inviolate and the first and last letter of the law we were to live by. And schisms and heresies, bloody religious wars and persecutions, inquisitions and inhumanities have followed upon the fact that the bishops and presbyters of the new religion, after the Council of Nicea, could not agree upon an authentic biography (among the many they had) and so gave the Christians four quite different ones as canonical, none of which was to be doubted or disbelieved by the faithful under pain of excommunication or worse, usually worse.

WHEN an ingenuous rational human being is asked to believe two opposed ideas concurrently under pain of damnation or death he is, usually, for a time, quite at a loss to make up his mind. He would like to believe, but he cannot believe two things that cancel each other. He may be ready to believe that "black is white" or "white is black," but, such are the simple processes of his mind, he cannot believe that "black is white, "white is black," "white is white" and "black is black" all at the same time. These gymnastics of credulity are beyond him.

If he is of a cunning and deceptive nature, used to

keeping counsel with himself against the outrageous furies of an entrenched, coercive and powerful majority, he will give lip service (in order to escape the rack, or in order to exist in peace, or in order to keep intact his immortal common sense and self-respect) to whatever nonsense is desperately required of him; and he will deepen daily in a cynicism toward the motives, minds and good intentions of all people who insist that other people believe and act exactly as they do.

If, on the other hand, he is at once a credulous and deductive creature, he will figure out that one of the two combative notions he is asked to believe in is the right one. And he will defend his conviction against all the forces combined against him. When this happens it is considered (long after it occurs and when poets and historians with poetical turns of mind begin to deal with the episode) to be a dispensation full of grandeur; but, nevertheless, it is an unpleasant incident, from both the physical and psychical point of view, to the martyr who is undergoing it. I have never been fed to the lions or had my limbs stretched on the rack or had my tongue pulled out by red-hot tongs or been burnt at stake, but I am quite, quite sure that I shouldn't enjoy any of these exhibitions of grandeur.

And I don't believe that any one else, who is not mentally deficient, has. Gavrillo Princep, who plunged us into a world war by his antic at Sarajevo, undoubtedly acted from what, to him, were the highest motives;

Czolgosz was proud to die for having murdered the amiable, incompetent and well-thought-of henchman of Mark Hanna, and his reasons must have seemed perfectly valid to him; and Giuseppe Zangara was pleased to burst into the limelight and have his pitiable, drab spirit extinguished forever by firing a shot at President Franklin D. Roosevelt which killed Mayor Cermak of Chicago.

We do not permit ourselves to believe that these men were quite right in their minds. That is to say, they were not right in *our* minds. But, at this distance, we may concede that the poor devils who gathered in the catacombs and on the campagna of Rome to worship a proscribed religion and were burnt at the stake or thrown to the lions for having done so, are martyrs deserving of our gratitude and of whatever sentimental reveries we can entertain toward them, whenever the incident is brought to our attention by historians or novelists or poets, whose work we happen to be reading while our wives are cooking dinner or when there is no good program on the radio.

One wonders what the gratitude of the present pope of the Holy Roman Catholic Church (baptized Achille Ratti in Desio, Italy, in 1857—he has a vested as well as a fiduciary reason for being grateful to the martyrs—), or the gratitude of Wolfgang Lumpenspiegel of Milwaukee, Wisconsin, or the gratitude of James-Jacques Aloysius Smith of Chickasha, Oklahoma, or the gratitude of Burton Rascoe of Larchmont, New York, means then, or now, to a young woman with a beautiful body and an energetic mind who was drawn by some emotional need (or because she had some splendid lover who could not earn a living under the economic inequalities of the Roman state and had taken up this promising Christian faith in a last desperate hope and had converted her to it) into an outlawed sect and had, in expiation, when caught and rounded up with other persons denounced by the police as Christians, been tied naked to a stake and burned for the sadistic pleasure of a drunken populace of the precise sort which enjoys a marathon dance or likes to throw pop bottles at an infielder who misses a grounder or at an umpire who gives an instantaneous decision (as, by rule, he must) when the decision is doubtful to other, prejudiced, eyes.

She, that lovely girl whom I see now agonizing in the flames, may have felt exaltation in her extremity. I have seen the coldest-blooded murderers on the death march to the scaffold singing hymns of the faith she died for—such is the dispensation of Providence or of a beneficent God or a kindly jailer with a hypodermic syringe, which makes the condemned, at the approach of death, anesthetic to the quick or slow misery they are about to encounter. But, with memories of a toothache, I don't think that they enjoyed that last agony, whether it be that paralyzing but painful shock of electrocution (as I have been informed by electrical experts this passing of the current through the body is) or this searing of the flesh from faggots lighted beneath one's feet.

I HOPE that, in the above, my intention is clear. I have tried to give a paradigm of the Passion of Our Lord Jesus Christ in some of its many varieties and analogies.

This story of the Passion is the one story that has touched the heart of humanity more than any other; for it is true to what people know of what has been done (usually in a lesser measure) to them and what they have done (usually in a slighter degree) to others. Existence is a competition and in this competition even the kindest, the best-disposed of persons sometimes commit cruelties unwittingly and repent of these cruelties if they ever learn of them. Usually they do not learn of them; and usually they repent of cruelties they haven't committed. In their beds at night they expiate in agony some phrase they have used in conversation which they think may have given offense to one of their listeners; and this is usually not the phrase that has really cut. Many wound with deliberation, but most of us don't: we wound almost incessantly without intending to; we wound by the mere fact of our existence and by our adherence to those dimly perceived aims we have in life.

The parable of the just man who is condemned to die is very old; for we all know that when we seek justice we are thwarted everywhere. So many conflicting opinions about justice! What may seem justice to you may deprive me of my liberty, my income, my sustenance or my life; therefore I cannot always agree with your definition of "Justice." That puts us in disunion; but, in the hearts of both of us, there is, apart from us, away from our own particular conflicts of ego, a real ideal justice to be attained. It is very unfortunate for you and me and all of us that in all our experience or in all our reading we cannot find a single instance where our ideal has been realized. Yet the belief persists and its constant defeat in reality gives glory to the Passion of Our Lord Jesus Christ.

The parable of the Passion, as we know it from the Scriptures and the Mass, was centuries old, perhaps millenniums old, before three of the least authenticated of the Four Gospels say a child was born to Mary, wife of Joseph, in a manger in Bethlehem in circumstances which gave rise to a reflection of two extreme points of view: the poetic and the nasty.

By this I mean there were some conditions surrounding the (later interpolated) story of the delivery of Jesus which gossips (and everybody is a gossip) subjected to different interpretations, according to their temperaments. One form of gossip held that Mary had been delivered of a child by divine conception while still a virgin, though long the wife of Joseph; that she had had a special form of intercourse with the Great God Jehovah (Yahweh) whereby she conceived and bore a child.

There were elements about this story which narrow-minded persons refused to accept. They were quite ready, it seems, to accept the story if it had said that Mary was an unmarried virgin. But Mary was married and what one knows about the conduct of the people from whom Joseph and Mary sprung (if one has read the frightful Old Testament) is enough to know that it is extremely unlikely that a Judean woman should be married many months and still remain a virgin; for rape, bigamy, adultery, fornication and sodomy seem to have been the chief proclivities of those people. Some seem to have had special vices such as eating shell-fish and pork. One wonders how they found time to tend their sheep, so libidinous were they, according to the sacred and authentic Word of God.

The nasty-minded therefore put the reverse interpretation on the story. You can leave the nasty-minded to do that. It humored them to say that Joseph was a cuckold. It was the pleasure of the nasty-minded to chalk up on the walls of the cathedrals, during the Middle Ages, the information that he was a deceived husband and to draw pictures of an ass with long ears and label the libel with either the name or the initials of our Lord Jesus Christ, just as in Paris it is customary to chalk up on the walls of an *école libre*, "*À bas* Ramsay MacDonald."

These tendencies are immemorial and perpetual with human nature—at once to exalt to godhead a man beloved by a portion of the populace and to make him out both a bastard and a fool. Apotheosizing and denigration are co-eternal in the minds of men. They happened even with the legends of so late a hero as Lincoln. With less tragic heroes, such as Alexander and Cæsar and George Washington, whose salvation was through works, not meditation, the tendency is to make them at once too perfect

for the incredulous to stomach or to make them such
monsters of depravity as any reliable physician would
explain is contrary to the most robust resources of virility.

Many serious and pitiable difficulties resulted from
the comparative stupidity of the Apostolic Fathers. The
Fathers would have been well-advised to leave off personal
prejudices against one another while they were establishing a religion and come to a common understanding. But,
obviously, each of the more powerful ones was fishing for
a see more powerful than his own and so, with the sees
of Antioch, Rome, Corinth, Alexandria, Carthage, and
Jerusalem represented, they made compromises with the
bishops from minor sees and so adopted four Gospels instead of one and threw out as "apocryphal" enough material as authentic as the accepted to make ten dozen
testaments. Thus they established as sacred, inviolate and
the word of God, transmuted through His most reliable
vicars, four biographies of His Son so disparate that it
has won Ph.D.'s for Biblical exegesists ever since and
has made militant atheists of millions of men, otherwise
pious, who like to argue.

IN adopting the canon of the New Testament the Apostolic Fathers were not guided by an irreproachable logic,
and confusion thrice confused has therefore resulted; but
they were guided by the shining virtue of literary taste.
Any one who has read the Apochryphal gospels, acts,
epistles, apocalypses, and "Sayings of Jesus," which are

now to be found in a compact volume, newly translated by Montague Rhodes James and issued by the Oxford University Press under the title *The Apocryphal New Testament,* will immediately be struck not only by the Church's rejection of the incredible for the implausible but by its keen sense of esthetic values.

I can recall but three instances in the New Testament as it is now constituted that offend my idea of the gentleness and delicacy of Jesus; and each of these instances may be the result either of a faulty translation into Greek of a lost original Hebrew text, and of a further destruction of the meaning when this text was rendered into English, or the result of pious interpolations.

Many commentators, reverential toward The Scriptures, have been shocked by the boorishness attributed to Jesus at the wedding feast in Cana, when the Holy Mother had merely said to Him, after the wine had run out, "They have no wine," and Jesus answered, "What have you to do with my work, woman?" The word in the Greek text is γυναι, the vocative of *gyne,* which means, in classical Greek, "woman," "wife," "female servant," "mistress" or "concubine," but never "mother."

Now it may be that in this instance some follower of Paul, who had no use for women except as instruments of relief for men and who was reluctant to acknowledge that women had souls, was far too zealous in furthering Paul's idea of women and therefore wrote into the original text a little idea of his own, whereby the Only Begotten

Son of God is made to be rude to His Sacred Mother. However, it is possible and even probable that the translator of the original Hebrew text of the brief and condensed gospel attributed to John made a slip (as translators sometimes do) and mistook the Hebrew *Aleph-Mem*, in this particular passage which means "mother," for *Aleph-Mem-He*, which means "woman," "concubine" or "female slave."

The other instances of a lapse of courtesy are: (1) when Jesus tells His disciples to take no food, bread or money and go into people's houses and camp themselves there until they are ready to go, and if any one refuse to let them in, to insult him by the gesture of shaking the dust from their shoes (*Luke* IX); and (2) when He said to the Samaritan woman at Jacob's well, "Give Me a drink," without offering to draw the water Himself, and in later colloquy with the woman said to her, "You worship what you do not know; we worship what we know, for salvation is from the Jews." (*John* IV).

Even if these passages are later corruptions of, or interpolations in, the earliest Hebrew or the earliest Greek texts, they still represent a slight error on the part of the Church in permitting such a delineation of the Savior.

But the huge mass of "apocryphal" matter, biographies, gospels, apocalypses, epistles, and sayings of Jesus, etc. (which purport to be the work of companions of Jesus or of eyewitnesses to the things reported or letters written by the original disciples, although some are as

late as the Fourth Century A.D.) contain so much fantastic
and distasteful stuff that it is a wonder that it won converts in the early days of the Church.

There is, for instance, the apocryphal Gospel according to Thomas, wherein the author, with the most pious
intentions, makes up for a deficiency in the other Gospels
by giving details of the life of Jesus up until the age of
five. Jesus is made out to have been an insufferable little
brat, cruel and vindictive. He was playing with some mud
in a puddle on the Sabbath, contrary to Jewish law, and
when another child told Him He should not play on the
Sabbath, Jesus told him He would wither him up like a
dead tree, and forthwith did so. A child, running through
the streets, brushed against Him, and Jesus said, "Thou
shalt not finish thy course," and the child fell dead. The
parents protested to Joseph, whereupon the child Jesus
said, "I know that these thy words are not thine: nevertheless for thy sake I will hold My peace: but they shall
bear their punishment," and "straightway those that accused Him were smitten with blindness." Joseph twisted
the lad's ear for this, "And the child was wroth and said
unto him: It suffices them to seek and not to find, and
verily thou hast done unwisely: knowest thou not that I
am thine? Vex Me not." (tr. James).

THE Apostolic Fathers would have saved their church
many difficulties if they had declared Matthew, Mark,
and Luke apocryphal and had used only The Good News

According to John (otherwise the Gospel According to St. John), the Acts of the Apostles, and the Epistles of Paul; for these latter items contain all the essential elements of the accepted Christian dogma, both Catholic and Protestant, including hatred of the Jews. There is no anti-Semitism in the Four Gospels, and, indeed, the four gospels were originally by, about and for Jews, and they represent the triumph of one sect of Jews over two other sects—the Essenes over the Pharisees and Sadducees, a triumph possible only after the destruction of Jerusalem by Titus, A.D. 70, and the reduction and dispersal of the Jews. Active anti-Semitism comes in with the Epistles of Paul.

II

Christianity in its earliest manifestation was a proletarian and religious revolution among the Jews; and by a quaint paradoxical irony, it had no sooner triumphed as a sect opposed to other Jewish sects than it became not only non-Jewish but actually anti-Semitic, though administered by apostate or semi-apostate Jews. As early as the close of the first century of our era, Justin Martyr, although inclined at first to admit that one might follow the laws of Moses and still be a Christian, explained that the orthodox position of the established church was that Judaized Christians could not hope for salvation.

Already, apostate Jews and Gentiles who had embraced Christianity were beginning to discriminate against

those Jews within their own fold who continued to practice the ancient ceremonies; they refused to have anything
to do with these Jews. Saulus, who signalized his disavowal
of Judaism by changing his name to Paulus (later to be
canonized as St. Paul by an organized and triumphant
Christian religion), in his Epistle to the Romans, is at first
a prideful Jew, asserting that salvation comes first to the
Jew and later to the other races, because the Jews are
circumcised and they were the first entrusted with the
oracles of God (*Romans* III). But later on he asserts that
all, both Jews and Gentiles, have sinned, and that salvation and eternal life are open to Jew and Gentile alike
if one but believe in Jesus Christ and obey God's commandments, in which the one Mosaic injunction, "Love thy
neighbor as thyself," sums up and embraces all the others.
Still later on Paul says that the Christians are the "chosen
ones," a "gracious selection" by God among the Jews, and
that a large portion of the Jewish race are lost to God and
can regain grace only by emulating the Gentiles who have
turned Christian. Still later he suspends the Jewish dietary
laws and asserts that "circumcision is nothing and uncir-
cumcision is nothing" and that the uncircumcised may
gain salvaton as readily as the circumcised if he keep
God's commandments.[1]

[1] This, it is claimed by some critics, is a concession by Paul to
expediency. Many pagans who otherwise were willing to embrace Christianity refrained from doing so because of the pain of circumcision. Circumcision had been immemorially the brand by which Jews distinguished
themselves from idolatrous races, as a sign of God's covenant with Abra-
ham, although there were periods in Jewish history when the practice of

It is curious to reflect that among Christian churches nowadays the Old Testament of the Hebrews is regarded as much the sacred and inspired word of God as the New Testament, whereas when Paul and Peter, Timothy, and James were preaching the Gospel and spreading the good news of the coming of the Messiah, His ministry, His death and resurrection as a redemption of all men from sin and as an assurance of everlasting life, they, the apostles and missionaries, held the Old Testament in disfavor and conscientiously followed Jesus' example in disobeying or disregarding the Old Testament laws, both secular and religious.

Jesus "profaned" the Sabbath, rejected the dietary taboos, and flouted the rabbinical rules against associating with publicans, fishermen, tax-gatherers and other lowly "untouchables." It was not until the earlier chronicles (the originals of which are all now lost) were beginning to be revamped for an elaboration of the Christian *mythos* which would gratify the taste for the miraculous among the superstitious pagans and also give to the proselytized Jews a sense of racial and religious continuity from the House of David, that the early scribes of the Church began to work into the existing narratives of Jesus and His teaching episodes designed to appear as fulfillments of Hebrew prophecies.

Because these ecclesiastical authors did not work in

circumcision was suspended. (See *Joshua* V, 2-9; *Exodus* IV, 24-26.) Circumcision was originally an Egyptian, not a Judean custom.

harmony or because there were individualists among them who had peculiar imaginative inspirations, the four accepted Gospels do not synchronize and only that of John achieved the extraordinary fancy of the raising of Lazarus from the dead, the embodiment of the Word and the dogma of the Only-begotten Son who is God's vicar on earth as well as His coequal in divinity.

In the miracle of John's inspiration there is a satisfactory mixture of the Greek myth of Orpheus, neo-Platonic philosophy, Mosaic prophecy, the dialectic of Philo Judaeus and Essene doctrine. It seems obvious that the author of the John Gospel was a cultivated and gifted Greek, a poet who was also erudite, a man of imagination and grace, because his is probably the greatest literary composition ever written—a prose work that has captured the hearts and minds of hundreds of millions all over the world and still continues to do so. In John alone is the Godship of Jesus clearly affirmed. St. Paul appears to have known nothing of the Godship of Jesus or of the Virgin birth. The incident of His resurrection Paul seems to have regarded as but a sign that all who were righteous and believed in God and the ministry of Jesus would be similarly raised from the dead and enjoy everlasting felicity.

THE verifiable origins of Christianity are veiled in an impenetrable mystery. We are really left almost with the alternatives of accepting the historical accuracy of the New Testament on faith and of reconciling its contradictions as common instances of human error (in which Jesus had no part, since He left no written record), or of rejecting the whole corpus as a pious fraud and imposture. It would appear that the faithful followers of the concept of the Gentle Jesus, who was the first God to be seen of men and to mingle with them, took care that we should have no other recourse but to accept one of these alternatives.

With two or three vague and minor exceptions there survive no contemporary references by non-Christian writers to Jesus or to the Christians, and of these few references they are either equivocal or believed to be later interpolations. It is generally argued that the early Church authorities proscribed or suppressed all non-Christian opinions and references to Jesus, lest they promote heresy; and this the authorities found it easy to do, once the dominion of the Church was established, because they were the only custodians and conservators of literary documents.

The most famous of all these alleged contemporary references is the isolated passage, having nothing to do with what goes before or comes after, in Josephus' *Antiquities of the Jews* (Chapter III, Book XVIII).

Now, there was about this time Jesus, a wise man, if it be lawful to call him a man, for he was a doer of wonderful works, a teacher of such men as receive the truth with pleasure. He drew over to him both many of the Jews, and many of the Gentiles. He was (the) Christ. And when Pilate, at the suggestion of the principal men amongst us, had condemned him to the cross, those that loved him at the first did not forsake him; for he appeared to them alive again the third day, as the divine prophets had foretold these and ten thousand other wonderful things concerning him. And the tribe of Christians, so named from him, are not extinct at this day.

Josephus was a Jewish historian, who wrote his *Antiquities* about 80 A.D. As Salomon Reinach points out, if Josephus had written that passage he would have been a Christian; "and as, since he was a Jew, he could not have written thus, he must either have said nothing of Jesus or spoken of Him in hostile terms which Christian copyists suppressed."

That the passage is an interpolation, however, is the more attested by the number of ecclesiasts after Origen (*circa* A.D. 230) until the fifteenth century who pointed to the passage in Josephus as non-Christian evidence of the existence and mission of Jesus. It is clear that the passage was not in the *Antiquities* that Origen knew because he does not mention it, although he very pointedly calls attention to the omission of any account of Jesus while citing Josephus' testimony concerning John the Baptist and James the Just, brother of Jesus. (Origen, *Contra Cels*. Bk. I.)

I would say to Celsus, who personates a Jew, that admitted of John the Baptist, and how he baptized Jesus, that one who lived but a little while after John and Jesus, wrote, how that John was a baptizer unto the remission of sins. For Josephus testifies in the eighteenth book of Jewish Antiquities, that John was the Baptist, and that he promised purification to those that were baptized. The same Josephus also, although he did not believe in Jesus as Christ, when he was inquiring after the cause of the destruction of Jerusalem and of the demolition of the temple, and ought to have said, that their machinations against Jesus were the cause of those miseries coming on the people, because they had slain that Christ who was foretold by the prophets, he, though as it were unwillingly, and yet as one not remote from the truth, says, "These miseries befell the Jews by way of revenge for James the Just, who was the brother of Jesus, that was called Christ, because they had slain him who was a most righteous person." Now this James was he whom that genuine disciple of Jesus, Paul, said he had seen as the Lord's brother, (*Gal.* i. 19.) which relation implies not so much nearness of blood, or the sameness of education, as it does the agreement of manners and preaching. If therefore he says the desolation of Jerusalem befell the Jews for the sake of James, with how much greater reason might he have said, that it happened for the sake of Jesus?

That the copy of the *Antiquities of the Jews* known to Origen did not contain the celebrated passage seems to me obvious from the above quotation; but it is also obvious that Reinach's conjecture that Josephus might have spoken of Jesus in hostile terms is not borne out by the above passage from Origen; for if the space now occupied by the questionable passage in Josephus was originally occupied by a denigration of Jesus, we may be sure that Origen would have controverted it.

From Origen to the fifteenth century no less than twenty-seven divines called attention to the spurious passage in Josephus as if to say that "Here is a Jew who testifies to the existence and divinity of Jesus; if you will not believe our testimony, at least believe in the testimony of a Jewish unbeliever." These arguments vary little in wording; and the citations, the weight of which rests largely on the words "if it be lawful to call him a man" and "This was the Christ," vary only in that St. Jerome translates the latter passage to read "He was believed to be Christ," and some others translate it, "He was called Christ," or, "He was Christ." The impious may conclude that it is a singular proceeding for the faithful to call so frequently to witness an unbeliever who, in their own eyes, is damned to eternal fire and brimstone.

ALTHOUGH Biblical scholars have lamented that there is no means (outside of the New Testament in which the accounts are at variance) of ascertaining the actual date of the birth and death of Jesus, the time of His ministry, or facts concerning His existence there is reason to believe (contrary to prevailing scholarly opinion) that we have a great deal of information from non-Christian sources about Jesus and the circumstances of His life.

I hold it to be probable that there were "Christians" before the time of Jesus, who is designated in the New Testament as the Christ (Χριστος, or the Anointed). The Christians, I believe, were a recalcitrant and revolutionary sect within the Jewish religion who revolted against the narrow dogmatism and religious formalism of the Pharisees and Sadducees who, for so long, dominated

Jewish laws and customs. The Christians were, I believe, the Essenes or a branch of the Essenes.

For an understanding of the complexion of the Jewish religion in the first century A.D., it is best to go to Flavius Josephus. In the XVIIIth book of his *Antiquities of the Jews* he says that for a great while the Jews had four sects of philosophy peculiar to themselves: the Pharisees, the Sadducees, the Essenes, and the Galileans. The Pharisees believed in the immortality of the soul, and that souls in after life will receive rewards and punishments according to whether they have lived virtuously or viciously in this life; however, they also believed that all things are determined by fate; therefore, they allowed all freedom of action to men as befitted their temperaments. The Pharisees, Josephus tells us, were the dominant sect, and were deemed to be most expert in interpreting the laws, and fanatical in enforcing them. They formed a clerical hierarchy, subject only to the authority of the high priest.

The Sadducees, on the other hand, believed that the soul dies with the body; they obeyed the letter of the law and the letter only; they were disputatious; they unwillingly took up civil office or service, and when they were forced to do so they compromised with the notions of the Pharisees.

But it is for the Essenes that Josephus reserves his greatest praise. They, he says, "teach the immortality of souls, and esteem that the rewards of righteousness are

to be earnestly striven for; and when they have dedicated
to God into the temple, they do not offer sacrifices themselves; yet is their course of life better than that of other
men; and they entirely addict themselves to husbandry."
He says the Essenes excelled all other men in virtue and
righteousness, and gives many instances to support his
assertion; he says they held all their goods in common,
no one having more than another; they had no servants
"as thinking having servants tempts men to be unjust";
that one branch of the sect did not marry while another
branch practiced marriage for the perpetuation of the
race, but both branches were continent and temperate
and ate in company out of a single dish; they did not
believe in oil for anointment but bathed in cold water,
and wore only garments of pure white; they despised
riches; they exercised mercy and charity to all alike,
whether of their sect or not, and were never known to
speak an ill word of any one, however hostile or vicious
that one might be; they refused to swear oaths, yet their
word was more binding than any oath; they honored God
first and Moses second; they respected their elders and
believed in the will of the majority; they were studious
and learned in medicine as well as in Mosaic law. Before
one was admitted into their order he had to undergo the
purification by water (*i.e.*, baptism, a later substitute for
the purification by blood sacrifice), and had to remain on
probation for three years to test his continence and his
adaptability to their ways of living. Then:

And before he is allowed to touch their common food, he is obliged to take tremendous oaths, that in the first place he will exercise piety towards God, and then that he will observe justice towards men, and that he will do no harm to any one, either of his own accord, or by the command of others; that he will always hate the wicked, and be assistant to the righteous, that he will ever show fidelity to all men; and especially to those in authority; because no one obtains the government without God's assistance; and that if he be in authority, he will at no time whatever abuse his authority, nor endeavour to outshine his subjects, either in his garments or any other finery; that he will be perpetually a lover of truth, and propose to himself to reprove those that tell lies; that he will keep his hands clear from theft, and his soul from unlawful gains; and that he will neither conceal any thing from those of his own sect, nor discover any of their doctrines to others, no, not though any one should compel him so to do at the hazard of his life.

That the Christian doctrine in its essentials was early formulated by the Essenes or by a branch of the sect is, I think, clear enough; for the communal spirit of the Apostles is reflected in the Gospels; the injunction to "sell all you have and give to the poor" was part of the Essene practice, as Josephus tells us; asceticism, chastity, temperance, forbearance, pacifism, mercy, charity, forgiveness for enemies and their ill-doing, disdain for riches and for the rewards of this earth in expectation of greater rewards in Heaven, meekness, humility, truthfulness, honesty and faith—all of these virtues, emphasized in the early days of the Church—were paramount in the idealism of the Essenes and also in their actual way of living, for Josephus tells us that, if any member of the order should violate his oath to obey their rules, he would be cast out and not permitted to reënter, as having violated the first of their requirements, that a man should abide by his word.

But it shall be my perhaps presumptuous task to show that the undoubted spiritual value of the Christian religion was an evolution and a manifestation of the hopes and aspirations of a people; and that while it was a revolution opposed to ecclesiastical dogmatism and to inflexible adherence to a dead past, it found in the usable past of the Jews an earnest of the deliverance of the Jews from an intolerable condition, in the shape of a warrior Liberator, Deliverer, or Messiah in kind like David of old; and that when such a warrior did arise and fought desperately and valiantly to throw off the Roman yoke and establish again a dominant Jewish kingdom, he, together with the more pacific among the Essenes, had to contend with the rich and dominant Pharisees and Sadducees who were content with the *status quo* and all too eager not to jeopardize their properties by an issue at arms with their Roman rulers; and that lastly when the revolution was put down, Jerusalem was razed to the ground and the Temple destroyed by the armies of Titus, this physical defeat was turned into a spiritual victory, and the hero or heroes of it were apotheosized and allegorized as the inspirers and founders of the most potent as well as the purest religion that has ever ap-

peared on earth,—a religion so pure that a practicing
Christian is a phenomenon in a multitude of professed
Christians.

"Less than a century after the Christian era, which
tradition places four years after the birth of Christ,"
writes Salomon Reinach in *A Short History of Christianity*,
"no one knew precisely when He was born, when He
taught, or when He died."

Yet, Reinach continues, some pages later on, "Christianity remains . . . not only a great institution, but
the mightiest spiritual force which has ever transformed
souls, a force which continues to evolve in them. Its influence is due partly to the beauty, now idyllic, now tragic,
of the legend, but still more to what is called the morality
of the Gospel, as revealed in the parables and sayings
attributed to Jesus. 'The spirit of the Gospel,' as Abbé
Loisy aptly says, 'is the highest manifestation of the
human conscience seeking happiness in justice.' It is true
that Christian morality is no more original than is any
other morality, religious or secular; it is that of the contemporary Jewish schoolmen, of a Hillel or a Gamaliel;
but in the Gospel it appears divested of all scholasticism
and ritualistic pedantry, robust and simple as befits a
doctrine setting forth to conquer the world. It is the
morality of the school without the school, purified and dis-
tilled in ardent souls, with all the charm and all the per-
suasive force of popular conceptions. It is not *social;* it
neglects the duties of man to the city, because it invites to

perfection, to individual purity, in the view of the Advent of the Lord and the Judgment, which were considered imminent even by St. Paul; but it prepares man to carry out his social duties by condemning hatred and violence and enjoining fraternity."

CHRISTIANITY was, in the beginning, a religion of the proletariat, the outcasts, the downtrodden and even of the criminal class. Paul, announcing in sermons and in letters the "Good News" (or Gospel) of the coming of Christ to redeem all men of whatever race, station or character from the curse of original sin and to procure for them by His vicarious sacrifice, redemption and life everlasting, was proud to designate himself, with more boastfulness than truth (for he was a man of substance, education and position), as one of the "riff-raff," contemptuous of the luxuries and pleasures and honors of a corrupt and material world. And to the ancient reproach of the pagan critics of Christianity that the Christians induced into their fold the lowest and most vicious classes of criminals, the early fathers were proud to assert that this was true; that faith had redeemed the criminals from criminality.

"The friends of Christianity," wrote Gibbon in *The Decline and Fall of the Roman Empire* (Chap. XV, Part III), "may acknowledge without a blush that many of the most eminent saints had been the most abandoned sinners. Those persons who in the world had followed, though in an imperfect manner, the dictates of benevolence and pro-

but as the Church grew and bishoprics grew or diminished in strength of numbers or in wealth from tithes and donations, envy and dissension, competition and controversy arose. The Church at Jerusalem, with much justice and some cogency, first sought to establish itself as the font from which all doctrines watering and replenishing the various churches should flow; for in Jerusalem Christ had held His ministry and had, according to the New Testament, died, and it was yet looked upon as the Holy City.

But the diocese of Jerusalem was impoverished and at precarious enmity with the orthodox Jews who were already beginning to calumniate Christ and the Christians in their Talmud in retaliation for the now overt anti-Semitism of the prevailing majority of Christian adherents. No sooner had the Greeks and Romans, and Gentiles generally, become the majority among the Christian converts than they began to hurl at the Jews imprecations for having "crucified our Christ," although there is no other instance in all history of the Jews having used the cross for execution—a Roman military form of death for seditionists and traitors. The Jewish manner of putting to death those convicted of impiety—they had no jurisdiction over malefactors, who were subject to trial only before the Roman governor or before the Roman courts—was by stoning.

The Roman diocese, by reason of its superior and increasing wealth and its dominant position, soon began to assert that dominance to which security and power always feels itself entitled. Learning much from the Roman civil organization and administration, the bishop and presbyters of the Roman church proposed to the other bishoprics that the government of the various churches should be vested in the bishop of Rome as the final authority, that the administration of the societies be directed from a central (Roman) authority, and finally that the vicarship of God should not be entrusted to too many, as provoking confusion, and should instead be vested in only one man, the bishop of Rome, who was to be the supreme pontiff and the infallible interpreter of God's will. There were competitive protests against this proposal by the ruling bishops of other cities but the power and wealth of the Roman communicants assured the ultimate sanction of their plan. Hence the Holy Roman Catholic Church.

FROM what tiny acorn grew this mighty oak? From a seed that no more resembles it than a cocoon resembles a butterfly. The seed was what an enterprising, well-educated, gifted, journalistically inclined and credulous young man named John Mark set down on papyrus as the story came from the lips of aged and illiterate Peter who had been a companion of Jesus. Tradition has it that Mark was secretary to Peter and there is considerable reason to accept the tradition, for even the revised and interpolated Mark that we have reveals the unmistakable traits of an amanuensis and a reporter, content to set down without comment or objection whatever was dictated to him.

The legend has it that Peter was a fisherman in partnership with James and John, that he owned his own boat and his own home and, in a relative degree, was prosperous, for his savings were such that he could give up his occupation to become a follower, and later a missionary of the doctrine, of Jesus.

But if the legend is true, he would have been unable to read or write, for education was only for those of the more prosperous classes and for those who were studying for the rabbinate. Peter would have need of a secretary who could not only read and write and converse in other tongues than Hebrew and Aramaic but who also could help him to prepare his sermons and his letters to missionaries to be read to heathen congregations, imploring them to become sanctified by baptism, repent of their sins, await the second coming of the Lord, and accept life everlasting.

Mark was Peter's man for this work. He was ardent as well as accomplished; and he was ambitious to propagate the "good news" himself, to become a man of prominence in the new dispensation. It occurred to him, we must infer, that Jesus had left no written words Himself, and that the spreading of the gospel had been hitherto by word of mouth. Peter was getting to be an old man. He was past middle-age, indeed, when he was selected by Jesus to be one of His followers. Mark, we still may infer, listened to Peter's account of the activity and ministry of Jesus, and set it all down faithfully as the old man remembered it and embroidered on it when he found his story accepted by a gaping and credulous audience.

To this Peter, who had known the Man called Jesus in the flesh, Jesus was the Messiah foretold by the prophets to deliver the Jews from bondage and to establish the Kingdom of Judaism over all the nations of the earth. This triumph was to be preceded by the destruction of the world as it then existed and by the death and resurrection of the Messiah himself, and, after this revolution had been accomplished (a new city growing upon the ashes of the destroyed Jerusalem), the Messiah would come again, destroy the world, and gather up the faithful ones in Heaven.

And to this simple Peter the Messiah was a deliverer of the poor and oppressed, the declassed laborers like himself, not only from the taxation and oppression of the Romans but from the even more onerous tyranny of the ruling caste of the Jewish religion. Peter hated the elders, the scribes and the high priests of the Pharisees and Sadducees who had ignored him and his kind, the lowly people; and whenever in the decline of his days and of his memory he could say something adverse to them, he seized the opportunity.

Nevertheless, Peter is at once a democratic and a practical man. In his trade these virtues are necessary for any modicum of success. He does not forbear to tell his young secretary, Mark, incidents which reflect upon his early infirmity of faith but which at the same time show that he is not accustomed to be taken in by anything. He confesses to having doubts at first about the Messiahship of Jesus (there had been so many false Messiahs of late, imposing upon the people); and he confesses with a pang of remorse that, in conformity with Jesus' prediction, he denied Jesus three times, for reasons of personal safety and expediency, and then was sorry for it, for Jesus was taken anyhow.

But even in this denial there is at once a certain boastfulness and a contention that he knew the Messiah in person and could attest that the Messiah so foreknew all things that he could anticipate Peter's denial of Him and still, with His understanding sympathy, not only forgive him, Peter, but hold him as one of the most cherished of his beloved apostles.

This simple Peter (and this ingenuous Mark) had no knowledge that Jesus was born of a virgin; nor did it concern them. The virgin birth was a discovery which came many years after the three-year mission of Jesus had ended on the cross, after all the eye-witnesses had died a natural death or the death of martyrs, and after pagan Greeks had been assimilated into the idealism of His mission and had begun to engraft pagan myths on the legend they had so zealously adopted.

Peter, through Mark, begins his account with the baptism of Jesus by John the Baptist in the Jordan and with the announcement of the revelation attending Jesus himself on this occasion to the effect that He, Jesus, is the

Man spoken of by John when he said, "One is coming after me who is more powerful than I, the strap of whose sandals I am not worthy to stoop and loose. I have baptized you with water, but he will baptize you with the Holy Spirit." (Reinach *et al.* are in error, by the way, when they assert that, although Jesus was Himself baptized, He baptized no one; for unless the passage is spurious John (III, 22) says, "After this Jesus and His disciples came into the land of Judæa and there He spent some time with them and baptized.")

The story told by Mark is very simple, concise, reasonably circumstantial, and to the point. The account disregards the antecedents of Jesus and the circumstances of His training. John the Baptist, a visionary, ascetic, and a prophet, after having long dwelt in contemplation of the prophecy of Isaiah ("Behold, I am sending you a messenger, who will prepare the way" and "Make ready the way of the Lord; make His path straight"), had reached the conclusion that he was the messenger and that the advent of the Lord was at hand. He preached baptism for the forgiveness of sins and baptized many in the Jordan.

Some mistook John for the Messiah, but he said that one was to come after him, the strap of whose sandals he was unworthy to tie; and presently there appeared Jesus of Nazareth in Galilee who asked to be baptized.

It is interesting to note parenthetically that there is

no town of Nazareth in Galilee and never has been. This
has puzzled the Biblical scholars not a little, especially
since the problem is complicated by the statement in
Matthew that Jesus was born in Bethlehem but that His
parents removed to Nazareth "that it might be fulfilled
which was spoken of the prophets, He shall be called a
Nazarene." The puzzlement of the scholars mounts to
dementia when they are confronted with the task of making sense out of an enigma whereby the parents of a child,
whom even in His mature years they do not understand
or consider to be a god, remove to a non-existent town
when the son is a mere baby, in order that an obscure
prophecy may be fulfilled. The trouble, it seems, arises
from the difficulty of translating Hebrew and Aramaic
into the proper Greek equivalent unless the one who attempts to do so is a thoroughly accomplished tri-linguist,
competent not only to supply the correct missing vowels
of the Hebrew but to find their exact equivalents in Greek,
and capable of detecting the phoneticized Aramaic in the
Hebrew characters and of rendering the result into under-
standable form. Those industrious and interesting scholars,
John I. Riegel and John H. Jordan, authors of *Simon, Son
of Man*, of whose real contribution to Biblical scholarship
I shall have occasion to speak later, point out that *Naza-
raios* in Aramaic means *the crowned one*, and not Nazarene; hence, according to John, XIX, 19, the inscription
on the cross was *Iesous ho Nazoraios ho Basileus ton
Ioudaion*, that is, "Jesus, the crowned one, King of the

Jews," not "Jesus of Nazareth," as it is usually translated.

According to Mark, who perhaps had the information from the aging Peter, John baptized Jesus and immediately Jesus received a portent in the form of a voice from the heavens announcing that He, Jesus, was God's Son, and therefore was the Messiah proclaimed by the prophets and announced by John the Baptist. Then, according to Mark, there was a singular action on the part of Jesus: knowing Himself to be the Anointed Son of God and, therefore, regnant over all the powers of evil, He permitted Himself to be tempted for forty days in the waste lands by Satan, whereas at any moment His power was such that He need only bid the Devil begone and that would be the end of the evil one.

(Riegel and Jordan, armed with linguistics and erudition, here rush in with a plausible explanation of this otherwise implausible occurrence: Jesus, and the Christ, they say, in all the Gospels, are but the cryptic names for the great Jewish war leader and distinguished rabbi, referred to by Josephus and profane writers as Simon Bar Gi'ora, who successfully waged war upon the Roman oppressors, harried the Roman legions, drove thousands of the Roman "swine" into the Lake of Gadara, and was finally taken prisoner through treachery, led in a mock triumph with a crown of thorns on his head through the streets of Rome into the presence of Titus, and condemned to be hurled from the Tarpeian rock near the temple of Jupiter Capitolinus.)

Then according to Mark, Jesus drew unto Himself disciples from among fishermen in Galilee and began His ministry. He taught in the synagogue in Capernaum and performed the current miracles and exorcisms which were common accomplishments among the magi of the time. All the while He cautioned His disciples not to betray the fact that He was the Messiah and the Son of God; and when He was directly questioned as to His identity He replied in an equivocal manner but nevertheless bade a paralytic to know that "the Son of Man has power on earth to forgive sins" and immediately thereafter revealed His identity by bidding the paralytic to "Rise, take up your pallet and walk," whereupon the man did as he was commanded.

Thenceforward, according to the testimony of Mark, Jesus continued to perform miracles, acquire followers, dispute with the Pharisees and confound them, violate the Sabbath to the consternation of the orthodox, preach in parables to a lowly multitude, associate with common men and eat with them without first washing His hands—again to the extreme consternation of the orthodox—and lastly to foresee that He was doomed as a scapegoat for the sins of man and that He would be betrayed by one of His disciples.

To Peter, James and John He gave an earnest of His divinity and His mission by taking them up on a high mountain where the voice of God came out of a cloud saying, "This is my beloved son, hear him." And Jesus

asked them not to tell any one of this until they had seen
the Son of Man risen from the dead.

Thereafter, Mark recounts the ministry of Jesus, records His sayings and parables as Peter recalled them and
depicts the betrayal and the Passion. To the revised
ur-Mark there were later added two passages, missing
from the oldest copies of the Greek New Testament, having to do with Jesus' appearance, after His entombment,
to Mary Magdalene and to two others who related the
experience to Peter and his companions.

THERE are some naïvetés in the Mark, which are perhaps
the result of a misguided piety on the part of later copyists. In Chapter Three we are given to understand that
Jesus' mother and His brothers were not aware of His
divine nature, in consequence of which they thought He
was "out of His mind" when He began His mission and
gathered unto Him a great multitude seeking to obtain
grace and to be cured of their illnesses.

This attitude on the part of Mary and her other sons
is perfectly consistent in Mark, because in Mark there is
no word of the Annunciation whereby she knew that she
was to bear the Son of God. In the other, and later, Gospels this attitude on the part of Mary would have been
inconsistent, for in them she was apprised of her unique
function. When Mary and her other sons came to take
Him away by force because they thought He was mad,
Mark has Jesus refuse to go out to them and also has Him

say, "Who is my mother and who are my brothers? Here are my mother and my brothers. Whoever does the will of God is my brother and sister and mother."

But later on in Mark (VII), when He is disputing with the Pharisees, He tells them that they obey the commandments of men instead of the commandment of God to "Honor thy father and thy mother." This is an inconsistency and one is hard put to discover why Jesus is represented, in effect, as denying His mother. The miracle of the loaves and fishes is twice performed in Mark, the variation being that in one instance twelve baskets were filled with the remains of the feast and in the other seven.

In Mark it is clear that the author's conception of Jesus is of a temporal as well as spiritual Messiah [3]—the liberator whom the Jews had long expected to deliver them from bondage to Rome, and to reëstablish the Jews in an independent kingdom which should ultimately triumph over all the other nations of the earth. This rather sanguine hope, as I shall explain later, was part and parcel of a tradition among the Jews which made them the most stiff-necked, intolerant and unsociable of people, and which caused them to be suspect even among the Phœnicians,

[3] "And he said unto them, Verily I say unto you, That there be some of them that stand here, which shall not taste of death till they have seen The Kingdom of God come with power." (Revised Version: *St. Mark*, IX, 1.)

The Riverside New Testament: "He said further to them, I tell you truly that there are some who are standing here, who will not taste death until they see the Kingdom of God already here in power."

who were Semitic, as well as among the polytheists of Egypt, Greece and Rome. It was a tradition that permeated Christianity even after the Gentiles were in the majority among Christian communities.

The "chosen ones of God," as the Jews arrogantly proclaimed themselves, were insensibly superseded by the "chosen among the Jews," which, in turn, again became "the chosen of God," *i.e.*, the Christians. The Christians in Rome became a civil problem no less than the Jews had been earlier; for the Christians refused to pay the slight head tax for the restoration of the temple of Jupiter Optimus Maximus (which had been destroyed by fire within a year after the destruction of the Temple at Jerusalem) because they believed it impious to recognize or pay tribute to a pagan deity.

The Christians of that era were sustained by a faith that, even if it did not move mountains, was a source of great perplexity among those Roman officials to whom experience had taught the lesson that those subject people are easiest governed who are legislated against the least. Severity and tolerance had been their watchwords and it was the imperial edict upon which all pro-consuls and procurators were enjoined to act: the provincial governors were to exercise lenience in all matters that did not interfere with the collection of taxes and with the administration of Roman fiscal rule. The Christians probably all too soon displayed an open contempt for the ways and means of the Roman state, and so brought upon themselves an obloquy that was attested in the martyrdoms of the faithful and in the writings of the pagans.

It must be admitted, however, that this protest against a head-tax was most demonstrative among those Christian converts who were least able to pay any such head-tax. The Christian doctrine of simplicity in living, disdain for luxury and riches, denial of pleasures, and contempt for the things of this world, were, indeed, factors which brought the proletarians swarming into the fold. As Gibbon says, "It is always easy, as well as agreeable, for the inferior ranks of mankind to claim a merit from the contempt of that pomp and pleasure which fortune has placed beyond their reach. The virtue of the primitive Christians, like that of the first Romans, was very frequently guarded by poverty and ignorance."

THE difficulty of establishing any historical authenticity to support the New Testament stories of the birth, mission and passion of the Lord Jesus Christ is admitted alike by ecclesiastical and secular scholars. For the impious and the skeptical there is perhaps a too persistent recurrence in the Epistles of Paul of the admonition to "believe." After a time this admonition begins to sound like an extramundane support of an entirely untenable series of data. And, on second thought, one realizes that this is the case. The reiterated appeal of Paul to those who would be saved is couched in a command; it is not in the form of the logic of the rhetoricians. It is as if Paul said, "What

I tell you is a denial of the evidence of your senses; but only by such a denial will you be led to the truth and be endowed with that grace which is the means of salvation." Therein lies the crux of that difference between the man who presumes to resolve the more heavenly mysteries in relation to himself and in relation to the world as he knows it and the man who accepts all phenomena as beyond his ken and, therefore, yields perfect support to whatever notions best fit his temperament.

The life, teaching and death of Jesus (even if He never lived, taught and died according to any of the records we have) remain the sweetest, the most tolerant, the most benevolent and the most universal of all dispensations in the form of religion. One may leave entirely to the theologians the intricacies and subtleties of faith; one may admit with the most virtuous of atheists (and most atheists are inordinately virtuous) that there are many discrepancies in the testimony concerning Him whom Christians revere. But in the very heart of all of us there is a condign conception of physical grace, irrespective of all spiritual accretions, that leads us to support the high idealistic conception of the Savior as it is set forth in the very faulty, contradictory, and incredible testimony of the New Testament. The simple subscribers to the faith were vindicated: Christianity swept and embraced all western Europe and permeated the ultimate regions of the earth.

The first and second centuries A.D. were an age of miracles, of which the Christians by no means had a monopoly. Although there is no single instance of Jesus or any of His disciples or of any one of the saints having asserted of himself that he could perform miracles, there is no end of testimony on the part of those who allege they were witnesses to miracles performed by others. In the Mark of the New Testament (VIII, 22-26) we are told that in Bethsaida Jesus encountered a blind man who begged Jesus to touch him. "And He took the blind man, and led him out of the town; and when He had spit on his eyes, and put His hands upon him," the man's eyesight was restored.

This same miracle is alleged (Tacitus, Book V, Chap. X) to have been performed by the Emperor Vespasian: "A certain man of the vulgar sort at Alexandria, well known for the decay of his eyes, kneeled down before him (Vespasian), and begged of him to cure his blindness, as by the admonition of Serapis, that god which this superstitious nation worships above others. He also desired that the emperor would be pleased to put some of his spittle on the balls of his eyes. Another infirm man there, who was lame of his hand, prayed Cæsar, as by the god's suggestion, to tread upon him with his foot. Vespasian at first began to laugh at them, and to reject them and when they were insistent with him, he sometimes feared he should have the reputation of a vain person, and sometimes upon the solicitation of the infirm, he flattered himself, and others flattered him with the hopes of succeeding. At last he ordered the physicians to give their opinion, whether this sort of blindness and lameness were curable by the art of man or not. The physicians answered uncertainly, that the one had not his visual faculty utterly destroyed, and that it might be restored: that the other's limbs were distorted, but if any healing virtue were made use of, they were capable of being made whole. Perhaps, said they, the gods are willing to assist, and that the emperor is chosen by divine interposition: however, they said at last, that if the cures succeeded, Cæsar would have the glory; if not, the poor miserable objects would only be laughed at. Whereupon Vespasian imagined that his good fortune would be universal, and that nothing on that account could be incredible, so he looked cheerfully, and in the sight of the multitude, who stood in great expectation, he did what they desired of him: upon which the lame hand was recovered, and the blind man saw immediately. Both these cures are related to this day by those who were present and when speaking falsely will get no reward."

Suetonius and Dio Cassius also testify to the miraculous cures performed by Vespasian [4] And according to

[4] In the important Old Russian translation of the *History of the Jewish War* by Josephus, discovered in 1906 (and to which I shall refer again later), there is a passage which states that among the Jews who awaited the coming of the Messiah there were some who believed "it meant Herodes, others the crucified miracle-monger (Jesus), others Vespasian."

To this testimony we must add, and contrast, the passage from

Philostratus in his life of Apollonius of Tyana (a biography based upon an earlier biography by Damis, who was a disciple of Apollonius) that holy man and magician, who had been instructed by the magi of India, raised from the dead a bride who had died at the moment of her marriage; cast out devils and unclean spirits; cured leprosy, dropsy, blindness, hydrophobia, lameness, and withered hands; transported himself thirty-five miles in the flicker of an eyelash to wipe out the plague in Ephesus; had the gift of foresight and prophecy; stopped in the middle of a discourse in Ephesus to tell his audience of the murder, at that precise moment, of Domitian by his freedman, Stephen, in Rome a thousand miles away; and finally ascended into heaven, later to reappear to one of his disciples in order to convince that doubter of the immortality of the soul. So great was the number of followers of Apollonius who revered him as a god that when Hierocles drew a parallel between the life of Christ and the life of Apollonius, Eusebius thought it incumbent upon him to denounce Philostratus for impiety, plagiarism and slander and to depict Apollonius as Anti-Christ.

Suetonius (Vesp. 4) which relates that when Vespasian was sent by the Emperor Claudius to become governor of Judæa he learned: "There had been spread throughout all the East parts an opinion of old, and the same settled in men's heads and constantly believed, that by the appointment of the destinies about such a time there should come out of Judæa those who were to be lords of the whole world; which being a prophecy (as afterwards the event showed) foretelling of the Roman emperor, the Jews drawing to themselves rebelled, and having slain the president there, put to flight also the lieutenant-general of Syria (a man of consular degree) coming in to aid, and took from him the eagle."

IT should be explained that I am one of those unfortunate beings who are skeptical of all phenomena that may not be perceived through the senses and accounted for in physical or chemical terms. That is to say (and I confess it freely), I am deficient in the very happy quality of faith in the miraculous and supernatural. I perceive miracles of nature all about me; I believe that all animate things, even trees and flowers, as well as the lower animals, birds and fishes are, in varying degrees, sentient; and I have just this moment been witness to the miracle of the birth of five kittens to my Maltese cat and to their demonstration (before my very eyes) of the quality we call instinct, for these kittens had no sooner emerged from their mother's womb than they sought and found her breasts to suckle; I know that birds and small animals may be made friends with if their fear is gradually overcome by gentleness and kindness and they come to have confidence in you, and in this I am supported not only by my experience but by the testimony of Dr. Gustav Eckstein who has made friends with white mice, cockroaches, canaries, a macaw, a turtle and other creatures. I have only to look at a slide under a microscope or glance at the heavens at night or to listen to a program coming in over the radio, to know that there are mysteries I shall never fathom and that may never be explained to the very last of my descendants. I know, too, that illnesses and diseases or the symptoms of illnesses and diseases (which amounts to the same thing) have sometimes been brought upon the victim by a confused or distressed mental state, and that these illnesses and diseases have vanished when the circumstances causing these distressed or confused mental states are removed. I have seen ignorant "faith healers" remove pain as if by magic through the faith or confidence of the patient; and for others I have known the efficacy of prayer (when the prayer is not of greed or of satisfaction of vanity) and I know the therapeutic value of confession. But I remain skeptical of the profounder prodigies that are reported concerning those who are of, or have assumed the flesh of, human beings.

In contrast to myself I may posit a sincere and very gifted man, the late Sir Arthur Conan Doyle, whose belief in spiritualism was not a matter of faith but of conviction, and, to him, of demonstration. He was quite convinced that he had communications with the dead and that the dead performed for him various parlor tricks which do not bear happy witness to the state of mental development we attain after we have shed the trappings of flesh and sinew and the troubles of this life. Sir Oliver Lodge, too, a physicist of renown, did not doubt that he received messages from his son, Raymond, who died during the World War. Nor did either of them accept the frank statement of Harry Houdini, who performed some of his most stupendous tricks before them, that what he had done was a deception which he was not privileged to reveal because he was a member in good standing of the Magicians' Association (members of which are pledged not to reveal their tricks to the public from whom they derive their living); but both of them and the entire body of the British Society for Psychical Research pronounced Houdini's tricks to be supernatural and impossible without supernal agency—a pronouncement which Houdini vigorously and vainly denied. One conceives that had Houdini been a charlatan and had he wished to propagate a series of ethical precepts, he might easily have become a god to hundreds of thousands of the credulous.

After I have said this, I acknowledge the right of any one to state that, after all, Doyle and Lodge may have been right and Houdini wrong; that Houdini (since he never revealed the physical nature of his tricks) may have been the instrument of a supernal agency without ever knowing it. And, having acknowledged this right, I accept and assert my deficiencies in the matter of accepting on faith all metaphysical phenomena.

The quandaries into which the New Testament, no less than the Old, throw the faithful believers in Christianity as well as dispassionate scholars are the result largely of two things: (1) the inadequacies of all existing translations, and (2) the literary method of *allegorical interpretation*, perfected by the Jews in the post-exilic period, and almost unknown in the literature of Europe. It is considered probable that the earliest Christian documents were in Aramaic or Hebrew or both. There are no vowels in the Hebrew alphabet and the translator of Hebrew into Greek is under the necessity of not only finding a Greek equivalent for the Hebrew term but also of correctly supplying the missing vowels. To do this correctly he would have to be completely bilingual. It would appear that these early translators were not always perfectly equipped for the task they undertook.

Allegorical interpretation (I take the definition from A. W. F. Blunt's succinct and scholarly *Israel before Christ,* an account of the Social and Religious Development in the Old Testament, published by Oxford University Press) means "that system of exegesis which treats stories not as narratives of supposed facts, but as moralizing tales, in which natural forces, moral qualities, divine activities, etc., have been personified under the form of human agents."

The New Testament is, by and large, I believe, a very superior example of this method of exegesis. And the first attempt at this form, with the intention of setting forth the new doctrine to which the name Christian became attached, was undertaken by the author of the original Mark of the New Testament. Biblical scholars, by the way, after much scrutiny of texts and manuscripts, cogitation and dispute, have arrived rather generally at the conclusion that the Mark that we have is the oldest gospel in the New Testament.

Their labors were unnecessary, for the author of the Mark tells us that his is the first of the narratives bearing the "good news of Jesus Christ." The very first words of the Mark are, according to the Revised Version, "The

beginning of the gospel of Jesus Christ, the Son of God"
(the last four words of this sentence do not occur in any
Greek text). The Gospel of Matthew is the product of a
school of thought which sought to give Jesus a Davidic
descent in order to conform with the early Jewish prophe-
cies of the coming of the Messiah; the Luke frankly
acknowledges antecedent authorities by beginning, "For-
asmuch as many have taken in hand to set forth in order
of declaration of those things which are most surely believed among us, even as they delivered them unto us,
which from the beginning were eye-witnesses and ministers of the word, it seemed good to me also, having had
perfect understanding of all things from the very first, to
write unto thee in order, most excellent Theophilus"; and
the John is a later and independent offshoot, deriving from
the earlier gospels but departing from them in important
particulars.

Now we must observe that nearly all biblical scholars
have noticed that, even down to the third century A.D.,
the Roman writers did not differentiate between the Jews
and Christians. When the pagan writers, such as Pliny
the Younger, Tacitus and Suetonius, referred to the Christians as disciples of a certain Christus or Chrestus, it was
as to a sect among the Jews who were especially obnox-
ious to the Romans, in that they were unruly, intolerant, clannish and disrespectful toward the Roman
deities.

It is my point that the pagan writers had no reason

to differentiate between Christians and Jews, because the early Christians were Jews, even before the concept of Jesus and His Passion was conceived, and that they remained predominantly Jewish in pride, in race, in intolerance, and in conscientious adherence to their many scruples even in the face of certain death.

Long before the Christian era, the Jews were in disfavor with all the other races in which they came in contact; for the Jews were eminently an arrogant and unsociable people. After the Dispersal and after the decline of the prophetic genius in the race, "the nation as a whole came to feel that the only course for them to take, until the creative spirit returned, was to practice themselves in strict obedience to the will of Yahweh. Hence the increasing emphasis on the letter of the law, and the increasing zeal for interpretation, which produced the scribal 'tradition.' This also had the advantage of ministering to that pride in their religion which, in the degradation of their outward circumstances, was the only resource left to them to preserve their national self-respect. If in every other way they were 'a worm' among the nations, in religious affairs at least they would assert their national spirit against foreigners. Thus grew the sense of separatism, and a spiritual scorn for the Gentiles, of which the New Testament gives constant evidence, and which finds perhaps its culminating expression in the words of II Esdras VI, 54-56: 'of him (Adam) come we all, the people whom thou hast chosen. . . . O Lord, . . . thou hast said that for our sakes thou madest the world. As for the other nations, which also come of Adam, thou hast said that they are nothing, and are like unto spittle; and thou hast likened the abundance of them unto a drop that falleth from a vessel.' " (Blunt: *Israel.*)

It is natural enough, therefore, that in time the Jews should have been looked upon as a despised race in sheer reprisal by those peoples whom they had shown no hesitancy in despising and likening to spittle. Expediency tempered the severity of Roman rule and the later, clement emperors, profited by the trials and errors of their predecessors in the matter of governing their alien subjects, displaying to the latter an urbane respect for their religious observances and their peculiar modes of living (however they may have differed from the Roman mode); and one Roman emperor asked the Jews that sacrifices and prayers be offered up, according to the Jewish ritual, in the Temple at Jerusalem to propitiate his reign.

The Jews accepted this request as a tribute to the efficacy of their rites; but, on any recorded occasion whereupon they were called upon to acknowledge or show respect for the pagan deities, the Jews declined to do so, vehemently, and on several occasions broke out in open rebellion. The Mosaic law which forbade the Jews to make any graven image was understood, even in New Testament times and later, as an injunction against any representation of human beings in any form of the plastic arts; and when the Roman legions bearing statues of Caius

Cæsar Caligula, who had deified himself, marched into Jerusalem under Caligula's orders that his statue be set up in the Holy Temple, the Jews were horrified at this "blasphemy" and "desecration." They protested to the Roman General, Petronius, who at first tried to be adamant. He told them that whatever their beliefs might be, he was, after all, responsible to his emperor for the carrying out of his emperor's orders. They told him, then, to run them all through with the sword and to gut the Jewish populace, since death was preferable with them to this "profanation."

The procurator thereupon told the Jews that he would obey their requests, remove the objectionable emblems, and assume responsibility in case the emperor should deem him negligent, deprive him of his post or demand his head. Meanwhile the procurator wrote to his sovereign, in effect, "Look here, we've got to go slow with these crazy idiots, these Jews in Palestine. They won't let the emblem of you come into their city as a deity and they are incensed that the soldiers stacked these emblems against the walls of their Temple. It is not that they have anything against you in particular, but they don't like the idea. They have one god, Yahweh, and they acknowledge no other gods. I have given them respite from execution until I have conferred with you; but, between you and me, I should suggest that we should yield to them as much as is compatible with the accruance of our revenues. If we slay them to a man, who is to tend the fields, who is to make money by usury, who is to pay us tribute for the maintenance of our hegemony?"

The Jews triumphed.

Meanwhile, and long antecedent to this, Jews had formed about one-fifth of the population of Rome. Because of their antisocial character they had been segregated across the Tiber in a community resembling the later Ghettos. Within this community there arose dissension, as always happens among argumentative peoples: the whole community believed in the imminent coming of a Messiah who should deliver the Jews from taxes to foreign monarchs, and who should establish a Jewish reign over all the races of the earth. This Liberator, according to old Testament prophecy, should be Χριστος, that is, the Anointed one of God. The Christians, that is to say those who believed that this event was to take place within their own memory, were at odds with the orthodox Jews who believed that the Messiah would come but at some far-distant and imprecise date.

The theory I am about to expound is not my own but is derived in part from an ingenious and fascinating book which I mentioned early in this chapter. The book is *Simon, Son of Man,* by John I. Riegel and John H. Jordan, published in 1917 by Sherman, French & Company of Boston. The theory of the Messrs. Riegel and Jordan received curious confirmation in Lion Feuchtwanger's *Josephus,* a fictionized biography of the great Jewish historian.

Although Feuchtwanger nowhere mentions Jesus or the Christ, it would seem that he also shares the view of Riegel and Jordan that the New Testament stories of the life of Jesus are allegorical interpretations of the career of the Jewish general and chief zealot, Simon Bar Gi'ora, who for three years successfully defied the Roman legions and was finally taken prisoner and executed after the fall of Jerusalem.

Reinach has remarked that the Crucifixion remains a tragedy without a cause. "The current belief that the Roman governor merely ratified a sentence pronounced by a Jewish tribunal is manifestly absurd. The Gospel narrative combines two traditions, one attributing the sentence to the Romans, the other (probably more recent) to the Jews. But if the Jews had condemned Jesus, He would have been stoned, crucifixion being unknown to Hebrew law. Now if Pilate caused a freeman to be scourged, he must have had for that some more serious reason than the alleged pretense of Jesus to a Messiahship, a thing that was of no concern to him."

But when the hypothesis is entertained that the history of Jesus, as it is related in the New Testament, is an allegory having to do with the career of a great insurrectionist leader so beloved by the Jews that they were willing to die at their own hands for him, we can see that the crucifixion was indeed a tragedy with a cause. The last great war of the Jews against the Romans lasted three and a half years, a period that corresponds with the

legendary period of Jesus' ministry. Simon Bar Gi'ora
(Bar Gi'ora means "Son of Man") was of the party of
Zealots and for this reason he was opposed by the Sadducees and Pharisees; but even from the inimical account
of him by Josephus we know that he had the devotion of
the great mass of Jews.

"In spite of all of his vilification at the hands of
Josephus," wrote Riegel and Jordan, "the fact stands out
that Simon Bar Gi'ora was a man of intense, almost re-
sistless energy. He swept like a devastating hurricane
across the hills of Idumea and the valleys and plains of
Judea. For three and a half years ('forty-two months' or
'1260 days') he kept at bay the greatest army that the
broad empire of Rome could furnish, and more than once
cut into 'fragments' and drove the soldiers like swine by
thousands into the sea."

Flavius Josephus was governor of Galilee in the years
A.D. 66 and 67, and it seems singular that he does not mention the Jesus we know from the New Testament, although he mentions Jesus, the son of Daneus, Jesus, the
son of Sapphias, Jesus, the son of Gamala, Jesus, the son
of Gamaliel, who were high priests; Jesus, son of Ananus,
Jesus, son of Thebuthus, high priests and revolutionary
generals in New Testament times.

"Josephus," wrote Riegel and Jordan, "covers every
phase of Jewish history and every movement of any moment that occurred in Palestine from Creation to his own
day, (yet) he lets drop no words which would raise a suspi-

cion that he had ever heard of a person called Jesus Christ. Still, according to the Gospels, tens of thousands of people followed Jesus from one end of the country to the other."

According to Josephus, Simon Bar Gi'ora on the occasion of his triumphal entry into Jerusalem, after his defeat of the Roman armies in Kadesh, was proclaimed "King of the Jews" by the populace, who looked upon him as the Messiah, whose coming was announced by the prophets. When, however, the armies of Titus finally overcame the city, Simon Bar Gi'ora, his son Eleazar (whom Riegel and Jordan identify with the Peter of the Gospels), and his lieutenants were taken prisoner.

Simon, as we know from Josephus, was taken to Rome in chains, and on his entrance to the city a mock triumph was arranged, wherein he was crowned with a crown of thorns and later executed before the temple Jupiter Capitolium as the climax of Titus' own pompous triumph. The Capitolium was so named, according to Riegel and Jordan, because workmen while excavating for the site of the temple of Jupiter found the head (*caput*) of a certain Olus. Hence the "place of the skull of Olus." In the Mark gospel the crucifixion was said to have occurred on Golgotha, which is, being interpreted, "the place of the skull." There has never been any place in or near Jerusalem called Golgotha or *Gulgoleth* (which means "skull" in Hebrew), and the conjecture of scholars that it was a place of execution named from the accumulated skulls of criminals is untenable because Jewish law forbade the exposure of any part of the human body after death.

I see no cogent reason for following Riegel and Jordan's contention that Simon was not crucified but was hurled from the Tarpeian Rock, because crucifixion, as Josephus testifies, was the common punishment meted out to the insurrectionist Jews by the Roman authorities. But their explanations of their other contentions, with citations from the New Testament stories, are highly ingenious.

One point they make in their contention that Simon or Jesus was not executed in Jerusalem is supported by the New Testament itself. In the New Testament stories, Jesus is represented as crying out in his last extremity, "Eli! Eli! lama sabachthani?" These are Aramaic words usually translated as "My God! My God! why hast thou forsaken me?" But those who had gathered to witness the execution are represented as not understanding what the words meant. Aramaic was the language commonly spoken in Jerusalem, and it is inconceivable that any group would have failed to understand these words if the execution had taken place in or near Jerusalem. In Rome, however, the Aramaic words would not have been understood.

Riegel and Jordan assert that the Pilate of the New Testament is not the name of the procurator of Judea, who had died nearly thirty years before, but that it is a corruption of the Roman word, *prælatus,* a judge who presides in a secular trial. In the original text the word is, indeed, ὁ Πείλατος and only in the Luke is this Peilatos given the first name of Pontius.

Riegel and Jordan also give a circumstantial account of the famous betrayal, attributed by the Gospels to Judas Iscariot. As it stands in the Gospels, this betrayal is highly incredible; for there is no warrant to it. Jesus and His followers in the Biblical story are known to the Roman authorities as well as to the high priests who denounced them; they had moved freely and their whereabouts were no secret. But, as a revolutionary leader, Simon, Son of Man, would have been sought with his followers for punishment.

These conjectures of Riegel and Jordan have great plausibility and make it possible for me to read the New Testament with a fuller understanding. After the destruction of Jerusalem by Titus, the razing of the temple and the utter subjection of the Jews, it would have been unwise for the Jewish historians and followers of Simon Bar Gi'ora to celebrate him under his own name, or even to write an allegory concerning him without setting the events they related at a period earlier than that in which they occurred.

How dangerous an accurate history would have been is readily to be seen by Josephus' account of the Jewish insurrection against the Romans; for Josephus, writing for the Romans, submitted his book to be edited by Vespasian and Titus and in it he vilified the Jewish leaders. There is, indeed, reason to suspect that Josephus is represented in the New Testament stories in the metaphorical rôle of Judas Iscariot.

It seems probable to me that the idealistic figure of Jesus is a composite portrait of Simon, his son Eleazar, Justus of Tiberias, and possibly zealous believers in the coming of ὁ Χριστος (the Christ) and in his reëstablishment of the Kingdom of God, with the Jews dominant among all races. We know from Josephus that Justus of Tiberias "incited the multitude to revolt, for his abilities lay in popular preaching, in invective against his opponents, and in the seductive witchery of his words, for he was not inexpert in the culture of the Greeks. Confident of that skill he set his hand to write a history of the Revolt for the purpose of covering up the truth." Riegel and Jordan suggest that Justus is the Paul of the Epistles. And I think there is much to bear them out.

I spoke a moment ago of an unidentified fourth figure from whom the earliest New Testament writers may have drawn the story of Jesus. This figure may have been the Gentle Jesus of tradition, the inspirer of the finer sentiments of the New Testament. If this is so, the historicity of the baptism, mission, teaching, trial and crucifixion of Jesus in the New Testament, shorn of the later additions and interpolations, is established. This Jesus antedated by a few years Simon Bar Gi'ora, Eleazar and Justus, and it is reasonable to conjecture that they were among His disciples.

The crucifixion of this Jesus *did* occur during the

reign of Pontius Pilate. In the Old Russian text of Josephus' *History of the Jewish War,* referred to above, there are these two passages (translated into French by Salomon Reinach and rendered into English by Florence Simmonds, in *Orpheus,* 1930):

Jew. War, II, IX, 3: At this time appeared a man, if indeed I may call him so, because, though human in form, he accomplished things more than human, thanks to some invisible power [Jesus not named; something must have been said about his parents and possibly his physical appearance, but that was erased]. Some thought that he was our first legislator [Moses] come to life again, others that he had been sent by God. For my part, knowing what I do, I would not say that, for he transgressed our Law on many points and did not observe the Sabbath according to the rules of our ancestors. But he did nothing shameful nor wicked; acting only through [magic] words. Many people followed him and accepted his teachings; many were moved by the hope that he would free the Jews from the Roman yoke. His usual abode was on the Mount of Olives, where he healed the sick. About 150 followers and a great many more poor people gathered around him. Seeing the power of his words, they exhorted him to enter the town, kill the Roman soldiers and Pilatus, and assume authority. But when the foremost Jews heard of that, they said to the High Priest: "We are really too weak to fight the Romans. But as the danger is also one for us, we must inform Pilatus. If he learns what is going on from another source he will bespoil or kill us, and disperse our children." Pilatus, warned by those Jews, sent soldiers who killed many of the mob and arrested the worker of cures. Pilatus had him tried and crucified according with [Roman] custom.

Jew. War, II, XI, 6: At this time (about 46 A.D.) many people showed their allegiance to the miracle-monger mentioned above; they said that this rabbi was still alive, though he had died, and that he would free them from servitude. A number of people listened to them; they all belonged to the class of artisans, such as cobblers and the like. The governor consulted with the scribes and, fearing that the movement would spread, sent some of those people to the emperor, others to Antioch for judgement, others to the places they came from.

It will be recalled that the spurious reference to Jesus occurs in Josephus' *Jewish Antiquities,* whereas this reference (although the name has been erased or omitted from the text) occurs in a translation of a *History of the Jewish War* by Josephus which is radically unlike the version we have. Josephus tells us that he wrote an earlier version of the *History* in Hebrew (the version we have is in Greek). That earlier version was written when Josephus himself was a young Jewish revolutionary and before he turned traitor to his cause when he was captured by the Romans, and, to escape crucifixion, became sycophant to Vespasian. The authenticity of the passages in the earlier *History* is obvious in every line. The first version was written for Josephus' own people; the second for the Romans.

These passages tend to support Riegel and Jordan's contention that the authors and editors of the earliest Gospels excoriated Josephus under the fictional character of Judas Iscariot. This is in accordance with the custom of the earliest Judeo-Christian scribes to write in allegory.

After the disastrous defeat of the Jews which resulted in the destruction of Jerusalem, it became necessary for them to say nothing in their writings against their

conquerors, lest they bring further misery upon themselves
and their people. Hence the New Testament exculpation
of Pontius Pilate and the attribution to Jesus of the saying, "Render unto Cæsar the things that are Cæsar's and
unto God the things that are God's" (that is, "Pay the tax
demanded by the Emperor; but keep your worship and
your conscience").

It is not strange that, after this persecuted small
Jewish sect, called Christians, had grown great in numbers
there should insensibly come about a literal interpretation
of what was at first something in the nature of a secret
code of revolutionaries. Time passed; a new generation
grew up; converted Greeks, Romans, Syrians and Cartha-
ginians outnumbered the Jews; the original meaning of
the Good News was largely lost and stories were invented,
original documents were elaborated, and allegory was accepted as history.

PETRONIUS

PETRONIUS

*

WHEN Caius Cæsar Caligula acceded to the title of
Emperor of the Roman Empire in the year 37 A.D.
there was one thing that particularly disturbed him. The
Jews in Palestine paid the tribute regularly demanded of
them; they offered sacrifices twice every day for Cæsar
and the Roman people; [1] they were docile in all things
but one: they acknowledged only one god and that god
was Jehovah, whose impalpable existence was so sacred
to them that they would not speak His name or permit
any artist to conceive a representation of Him on canvas
or in stone or plaster. The readiness of the Romans to make
deities of their emperors, even when those emperors were
still alive, was an abomination to the Jews. However, they
did not protest against the practice except when they, as
Roman subjects, were called upon to acknowledge the Roman Cæsars as gods.

This they refused to do. In fact, when Pontius Pilate

[1] Josephus, *Wars of the Jews,* Chapter X, 4.

was sent by Tiberius to Cæsarea to be procurator of Judæa, the first difficulty he encountered was concerned with the peculiar religious customs of the Jews. In the military occupancy of Jerusalem, the Holy City of the Hebrews, he made the mistake, in his ignorance, of sending soldiers bearing the Roman ensigns (representing the deified Cæsar).

When the Jews discovered this profanation (the laws "do not permit any sort of image to be brought into the city"—Josephus, *Wars of the Jews,* IX), numbers of them hastened to Cæsarea and urged Pilate to preserve their ancient laws inviolate and remove the hated images from the city. Pilate denied their request, whereupon the whole delegation fell prostrate upon the ground and remained immovable for five days and nights.

Finally Pilate sat upon his rostrum in the marketplace and told the Jews he would give them an answer. Meanwhile he had instructed his soldiery to surround the Jews in three ranks. Then he told the delegation that unless they admitted Cæsar's images into their city without protest they would be slain on the spot. In one accord these Jews fell down, exposed their necks and cried out that they had rather die than have their laws transgressed. This was a stunner for Pilate and, on his own responsibility, he ordered the ensigns to be carried out of Jerusalem.

Caligula—who was so vain that he had himself deified on coming into power without waiting for the vote of the

Senate and people of Rome—must have heard of this; for one of the first acts of his reign was to send the commander, Petronius, with an army to Jerusalem with the express purpose of placing statues of himself within the holy temple. In doing this he went over the head of Pilate, who was still procurator of Judæa.

When Petronius and his army arrived at Ptolemais, which was the maritime city of Galilee, they were met by a vast assembly of Jews with their wives and children, who had been apprised of Petronius' mission. They petitioned Petronius not to carry out Caligula's order because it was a profanation to them. This was a puzzler to Petronius as it had been to Pilate: he was, no doubt, an easy-going skeptic and cynic himself, and it is probable that he had no illusion that the fatuous Caligula was a god; but it was inconceivable to him that faith in an unmentionable deity should be carried to such preposterous lengths as these Jews were visibly displaying before him.

Petronius told the delegation that their request was singular inasmuch as all other nations in subjection to the Romans placed the image of Cæsar among the rest of their gods. The spokesmen for the Jews patiently explained to Petronius that it was against the Jewish religious laws to make an image even of a man, least of all of God, or to suffer the presence of such an image in the most abominable part of their country, least of all in the temple itself.

Petronius replied: "And am I not also bound to keep the law of my lord? For if I transgress it, and spare you, it is but just that I perish; while he that sent me, and not I, will commence a war against you; for I am under command as well as you."

The multitude cried out that they were ready to die for their law.

Petronius asked them if they would make war against Cæsar, to which they replied that if he carried out his intention of putting the images in the temple he would have to sacrifice the whole Jewish nation, for they were ready to expose themselves and their wives and children to be slain rather than endure this blasphemy.

In the words of Josephus, Petronius "pitied them on account of the inexpressible sense of religion the men were under and that courage of theirs which made them ready to die for it." He dismissed them; but on the following day he conferred privately with some of the men of power among the Jews, arguing, cajoling, threatening them, with no success. Fifty days passed and no Jew did a stroke of work although it was time for sowing the crops. Petronius saw that the country was in danger of lying without tillage and so he called the Jews together and told them that he would take the hazard of Cæsar's displeasure upon himself, and try to reason with him. "In case Cæsar continues in his rage," he said, "I will be ready to expose my own life for such a great number as you are."

Petronius withdrew his army to Antioch and wrote to Caligula, explaining the whole situation, and saying that unless Caligula was prepared to lose all Judæa and all the

Jews in it he must respect the Jewish laws and countermand his order. Caligula lost his temper on reading this letter and wrote to Petronius rebuking him for insubordination and saying he would have him executed for high treason if he did not obey his command instanter. Fortunately, however, the messengers carrying Caligula's letter were shipwrecked and the letter did not reach Petronius for three months—or twenty days after he had received news of Caligula's assassination.

THIS Petronius served under Caligula's successor, Claudius, and later under Nero, becoming governor of Bithynia and later chief magistrate, in which offices he grew rich from his share of imposts and concessions, as was customary among colonial governors under the Roman empire. He seems to have been a man of taste and refinement as well as a man-of-the-world with tact and a sense of justice (as his encounter with the Jews reveals) and in his later years he appears to have recommended himself to Nero because of his qualities as a connoisseur, epicure, and artist in luxury, wherefore Nero made him "arbiter of taste and elegance" at the imperial court.

To this Petronius we have four references in the literature of his period—one by Josephus (all of the classical scholars who have written of Petronius seem to be ignorant of the work of Josephus), one by Pliny the Younger, one by Plutarch, and one by Tacitus which has fascinated many writers because of its uniqueness as a character sketch in ancient literature. In Greenway's quaintly readable, if not quite accurate translation, the passage from the *Annals* of Tacitus is this:

"Of C. Petronius ... he passed his day in sleepe, and the night in delightfull sports, or other affairs of life. And as others, industry; so this man, sloth had raised to fame; a riotous and wastfull spender he was, not accompted like many, which run through all, but using riot to his credit. And his words and deeds how much the freer, and shewing a certaine carelesnesse; so much the more gratefully received, as favoring somewhat of simplicity. Notwithstanding being Proconsull of Bithynia, and anon after Consull, he shewed himselfe quicke and stout, and able to wade thorow great matters. Then falling againe to his vices, or else shew of vices, was received by Nero who esteemed nothing pleasant or delightfull unlesse *Petronius* had approved it. Thereupon grew *Tigellinus* malice against him, as against a concurrent, or one more skilfull in pleasure than himselfe, whetting Neroes cruelty (unto which all other lusts gave place) against him: objecting the friendship he had with Scevinus, corrupting a slave to be his accuser: taking from him all meanes of defence, and the greatest part of his family drawne into prison. By chance about that time *Cæsar* went to Campania, and *Petronius* gone as farre as Cumas, was there stayed; and not able any longer to indure the lingering betweene hope, or feare, yet did not rashly kill himself, but cutting his vaines, and binding them up as pleased him, opened them againe, and talked with his friends, though not of any serious matter, or worthy to purchase the glory: but gave care to those which discoursed with him, yet nothing of immortality of the soule, or opinions of wise men, but of light verses, and easie songs. On some of his slaves he bestowed gifts, and on some stripes. He went sometimes abroad, and gave himself to sleepe, that although his death was constrained, yet it should be like a casuall death. Neither in his Testament (as most men are wont to doe) did he flatter *Nero* or *Tigellinus* or any other favorite, but wrote downe the uncleane life of the Prince, under fained names of stale calamities abused against nature and of women, with the strangenesse of the abuse of either of them; and sealed up, sent it to Nero, and brake his scale, least afterward it might serve to breed danger to others."

Now this Petronius is an alluring creature, surely, so heroic and self-assured, so urbane and disillusioned, so ready to accept misfortune with a shrug and meet death with dramatic levity. But the scholars have fixed on him the authorship of the most extraordinary masterpiece in Latin literature, the first picaresque romance in any language—*The Satyricon!* Hear Theodor Mommsen, as long ago as 1878: "The question as to the date of the narrative of the adventures of Encolpius and his boon companions must be regarded as settled. This narrative is unsurpassed in originality and mastery of treatment among the writings of Roman literature. Nor does any one doubt the identity of its author and the Arbiter Elegantarium of Nero, whose end Tacitus relates." And even so recent a translator and commentator, J. M. Mitchell (*Petronius, Leader of Fashion*, 1922), does not doubt that Nero's Petronius and the author of *The Satyricon* were the same person, despite the many objections that have been raised against such an identification. Moreover, most of the scholars accept the scholastic legend that *The Satyricon* is a satire against Nero, some of them even holding that the "testament" Petronius sent to Nero in which he catalogued the vices of the emperor and his favorites was *The Satyricon* of which we apparently have about one-eighth in fragments! Even the fragments bulk to the size of an ordinary novel. It is inconceivable that any one should have written it between the time he was ordered to commit suicide by Nero and the carrying out of the order.

This scholarly tradition is all the more inexplicable in that the author of *The Satyricon* tells us plainly that the events he depicts took place under the reign of Titus, who did not become emperor until eleven years after Nero's death.

In Chapter Forty-five of *The Satyricon*, the rag-man Echion is talking about a gladiatorial fight which has been announced to take place shortly. *"Et Titus noster magnum animum habet, est calidi cerebri, aut hoc, aut illud erit; notus utique; nam illi domesticus sum."* ("And our Titus has a great mind and a hot head; he will see that things are on the square; no frame-ups; I know because he and I are close friends.")² This is a free translation, but the reader must remember that here the author of *The Satyricon* is giving us a portrayal of a boaster. Echion is only a rag-man and yet he pretends to have the ear and confidence of the emperor. He has some menial job in the emperor's household and so he tells his listeners—very illiterately—that he knows the emperor intimately and can assure them that the gladiatorial fights will not be fixed. Echion is like Ring Lardner's bush-league baseball player, and his speech, like the "Busher's," is highly ungrammatical.

It is strange indeed that the idea should ever have become current that *The Satyricon* is a satire on Nero, because the Trimalchio of that novel bears no resemblance to the extant accounts we have of Nero. Trimalchio is an ostentatious and vulgar freedman, engaged in commerce and a member of the *nouveaux riches*. He is pictured as being old, bald and fat, and made to toe the mark by a husky, domineering and efficient wife.

Nero was never old; he died at the age of thirty-one. He divorced and put to death his wife Octavia in order to marry his mistress Poppæa Sabina, murdered Poppæa

---

² Echion's assurances are borne out by Suetonius who relates that Titus built an amphitheater wherein in one day he put five thousand wild beasts to be baited, and wherein Eusebius (Chronicles II) tells us ten thousand gladiators and other performers were slain in one event. Both writers were given to wild-eyed exaggeration, but Titus did stage gladiatorial combats and, as we know from Josephus, he was accustomed to do things on a vast scale.

in order to marry Antonia, daughter of Claudius, and, on being refused by her, caused Antonia to be murdered, and married Statilia Messalina. Such a career does not indicate that Nero was henpecked.

Marcel Schwob, that delicate and sensitive writer and scholar of great erudition whom Anatole France admired more than any of his contemporaries except Courtelaine, has written his version of what Petronius was like and what happened to him. It appears in *Imaginary Lives,* translated by Lorimer Hammond. It pleased Schwob to accept the tradition in part concerning Petronius. But he did this only in order to construct an ironical miniature. He says that Tacitus is wrong in saying that Petronius was at the court of Nero or that he committed suicide at the emperor's request: he was a rich man's son, well educated and with a taste for making verses; he imagined adventures such as are recorded in *The Satyricon* and, after he had read them to his slave, he sought the sort of adventure he had imagined in his novel:

"His appearance made disguise easy. Turn by turn, he and Syrus carried the leather sack containing their money and clothing. They slept in the open air, on hillocks beside the crossroads, often watching the dismal cemetery lamp twinkling among the tombs. They ate their bread sour and their olives rancid. They became wandering magicians, vagabond fakirs, companions of runaway soldiers. Petronius dropped his writing completely, for he now lived the life he had once imagined.

They had treacherous friends whom they cared for, he and Syrus, and who left them at the gates of towns after borrowing their last coin. They carried on all sorts of debauches with gladiators: they became barbers and scrubmen. For several months they lived on crusts stolen from the graves of the dead, and all who saw Petronius were terrified by his wry eye and the swart cast of him. One night he disappeared. Syrus expected to find him in a dirty hovel where he had been with a tangled-haired girl, but a drunken squatter had sunk a knife in his neck while they were lying together on the floor of an abandoned cave in the open country."

Inasmuch as we have no real information on the subject, Schwob's imaginary version of the life of the author of *The Satyricon* is as good as any other, perhaps, and is certainly better than the version derived from Tacitus. But I think that Schwob puts the cart before the horse. It seems to me that whoever wrote *The Satyricon* had had some of the experiences he describes before he wrote the novel. If there had been in Latin literature other picaresque tales before *The Satyricon* was written, a rich, young æsthete, such as Schwob imagines Petronius as being, might have had his imagination stimulated to imitate the sort of thing he had read and improve upon it; but *The Satyricon* was the first novel of its kind.

Moreover, I believe there is internal evidence that the author is speaking in his own person in the character of the narrator, Encolpius.

Although Encolpius is a scalawag, he is also a scholar and something of a poet. He is discomfited at every turn, but this never feazes him; and this I take to be the author's humorous exaggeration at once of his difficulties and of his ability to cope with them. The truly humorous writer always projects his plight into one of his characters and reassures himself on one hand while denigrating himself on the other.

Of course, all the characters that an author creates, hero or villain, heroine or slattern, are in a way autobiographical, projections of himself: the qualities of the hero or heroine may be those he aspires to and the qualities of the villain or the slattern may be those he particularly loathes; but, at the same time, he knows that they are features in his own make-up which he has felt deep in his heart, whether he has given overt expression to them or not. In all works of the imagination there is, I think, a character by whom one may identify the author's essential self or his humorous scrutiny of himself. In this character the novelist comes closest to laying his heart all bare and bleeding. Even if he creates an imp like Encolpius or like Tyl Eulenspiegel, there is pity in the portrait and in the warmth of this we forgive the rascal everything. . . . And so I think that, with the proper reservations and allowances for artistic exaggeration, we may find in the character of the narrator, Encolpius, in *The Satyricon* as much of a self-portrait, say, as that of Proust in *Remembrance of Things Past*.

The story of *The Satyricon*, the picture of life it gives, is not universally, but only intermittently, true to life as we know it. It could not have been conceived and written by an author who had been reared on the Island of Bali or by an author who had spent most of his years on an Iowa farm; but, allowing for some local differences in the shades of poverty and depravity, it could have been written by any one cognizant of conditions in London, Berlin, Paris, Brussels, Buenos Ayres, New York, Chicago, San Francisco or New Orleans—in fact, in any large capital of the world. It is not true to the life known and experienced by the presidents of Wisconsin and Princeton Universities (except, perhaps, when for matters of expedience, they have to have dinner with a donor to the university who is very like Trimalchio); but it is true to the life of Hell's Kitchen and the slums of Boston. And more importantly it is true to the realm of the imagination.

The Satyricon is the ultimate sardonic comment upon the civilization which Roman conquest produced. While I am unwilling to accept the tradition that attributes the authorship of the novel to the arbiter of taste under Nero, I am disposed to suggest that the son of that Petronius was the author. Nero's Petronius was much too active a man as soldier and colonial administrator to have had the experience, leisure and concentrated genius to produce that extraordinary medley of satire, picaresque romance, short stories, character portrayal and realism. The author of *The Satyricon* knew the slang, the idiom and the people of the Roman underworld. Nero's Petronius spent the major part of his life in Bithynia and Judæa; it is not likely that he would have known the ways of thieves, cut-throats, prostitutes, and threadbare poets and philosophers. His fastidiousness, if not his career, would have kept him from such associations.

The author of *The Satyricon* does, however, show a knowledge of the Near East that might easily have been absorbed by the son of a colonial governor. He mentions the Jewish rite of circumcision and other customs among the inhabitants of Africa and Asia Minor. It is to be supposed that the son of a Roman colonial governor was given the best education available at the time. He was probably taught by private tutors, learning Greek as early as Latin, and later sent to Athens to round off his education. With a father stationed in Bithynia until recalled to Rome by Nero, the younger Petronius might have opportunity and leisure to develop his literary talents. We must also remember that when Nero ordered Petronius to kill himself, he had already imprisoned Petronius' whole family and had issued the order for the confiscation of Petronius' property. (Pliny says that just before his death Petronius called for a gold cup which had cost him 300,000 sesterces and broke it lest Nero seize it.)

The younger Petronius then would have been left without a cent. Thrown upon the world unprepared for a career or a trade, it would have been logical for him to take up the vagabond existence in company with scalawag poets and philosophers such as are described in *The Satyricon*. As an observant son in a rich consul's house he would have had the opportunity to observe millionaire vulgarians like Trimalchio. (Tradition forbade Romans of equestrian rank and higher to engage in trade; hence the rise of a class of enormously wealthy freedmen who grew rich in trade, speculation and usury, whereas the military and civil officers depended upon the emperor for their share of booty and taxation.) It is further to be remarked that the author of *The Satyricon* says that genius is nourished in poverty and that "brains and poverty are twin sisters"; he deplores the decay of the arts in a society where "gods and men alike conspire to glorify gold above any production of those infatuated little Greeks, Apelles and Pheidias." These are sentiments Petronius Arbiter would not be likely to utter or approve of; yet they would be natural to his talented and penniless son.

The Satyricon was lost to the world for nearly sixteen hundred years and when it turned up in Dalmatia in 1663 it was in a highly mutilated condition, so mutilated, indeed, that two clever forgers, François Nodot in 1690 and José Marchena in 1768, attempted to piece out the lacunæ in the narrative and their "discoveries" were readily accepted as authentic by the great classical scholars of their periods. One does not have to draw invidious conclusions about the nature of the learning of these great classical scholars to applaud them for their innocence; for Nodot

and Marchena did, very cleverly, supply plausible matter
for the texts that were missing.

There is no perfect agreement among the savants as
to just what the word, "Satyricon," means, some holding
that it comes from the Greek word Σατυρος meaning
"satyr" (and by derivation "satire"), and others holding
that it comes from the Latin word *satura* which means a
medley, a hash, an olla-podrida and a dish on which various kinds of food were served.

One should minimize one's excitement over these
scholastic quibbles, because *The Satyricon* is both a hash
and a satire, a very piquant and flavorous hash, I might
say, and (in the part depicting Trimalchio's dinner) one
of the wittiest satires extant. It amazes me that no scholar
has suggested that the title of the book, as we have it, is
a copyist's corruption of the word *satyrion*, which is an
aphrodisiac. It is a word used all the way through the
book. Perhaps the author jestingly allowed that his novel
would act upon his readers like cantharides. Indeed, it
would seem from the mutilated state in which the work
has come down to us that some lover or lovers of erotica
tore out passages of special explicitness. The most famous
portion of the book, that depicting Trimalchio's dinner,
comes to us intact; but the escapades of the rogues
Encolpius, Ascyltus, Giton and Eumolpus are frag-
mentary.

The story opens with a discussion between Encolpius,
the narrator, and Agamemnon, a teacher, on literary and

oratorical values. This discussion by inference proclaims Petronius' literary aims and methods—the things which give life, verve and contemporaneity to *The Satyricon*. The reason for the decay of literature and oratory, he says, is that the colleges teach the wrong things and in the wrong way. In the schools, he says, the youngsters never hear anything touching upon the everyday things of life; all they read or hear is about "pirates standing in chains on the seashore; tyrants scribbling edicts in which sons are ordered to behead their own fathers; responses from oracles delivered in time of pestilence, ordering the immolation of three more virgins; every word a honied drop, every period sprinkled with poppy-seed and sesame." No wonder the youngsters never learn any sense or acquire any taste, fed as they are on such a diet, he observes. "With your well-modulated and empty tones you have so labored for rhetorical effect that the body of your speech has lost its vigor and died"; Asiatic ornament has corrupted expression and destroyed the grace and charm of natural style.

The two older friends, Encolpius and Ascyltus, quarrel for several chapters over the boy, Giton, and finally make up in order to go a-thieving when their money runs out. They steal some money, sew it into a raggedy cloak and then Encolpius, too intent on an amorous adventure, loses the cloak. They steal a mantle; but on their arrival at a fair they run into the people from whom they have stolen the mantle—and the man of the family is wearing their cloak! They find out that the money is intact and after much dispute, in which shyster lawyers try to get both garments, they effect an exchange.

These chapters depict actions that are particularly animalistic; but not once is there a suggestion that the author has a moral judgment in reserve against the ragamuffins or the nymphomaniacs they encounter. There is a dispassionate serenity and a quiet amusement in the attitude of our Petronius. He is completely amoral. His blandly ingenuous adventurers have no sense of sin, no conscience, no scruples; they appear to have no parents, no ancestors, no background except familiarity with the classics and an early training in adversity and hard knocks; they are callous and undismayed under discomfiture and the bastinado; they are as simple-hearted and undisciplined as children who have not yet felt the coercive force of society. They are free men.

Bernard Shaw once said, apropos of W. H. Davies (*The Autobiography of a Super-tramp*), that if he had the courage he would take to the road; for only in the life of a tramp is it possible to escape the restraints upon freedom that are everywhere evident in civilized society. Hoboes, whose freedom has been restrained in chain gangs by the laws against vagabondage and vagrancy in the states of this country where Work is held so sacred that in the year 1933 we have only 10,000,000 unemployed, would undoubtedly instruct Mr. Shaw in the drawbacks to their way of life; but, theoretically, the hobo is a member of the only class that has successfully evaded the responsibilities and restrictions in a competitive society.

The vagabond, especially if he is a roguish and talented one, exercises like the outlaw (especially if the latter's deeds occur in a romantic past) a perennial charm over the imagination of us duty-bound and provident folk. The vagabond represents to us a release from the prison of what is expected of us in the matter of toil and ambition, of regard for our neighbor's censure, of obedience to the shifting codes and faiths and of provision for an unpredictable future. The vagabond has the audacity to live only in the present, for himself wholly, without either fear or hope, taking care only to avoid entanglements with those symbols and executors of law and order—the police.

The Satyricon is the first great novel of the vagabonds and it still stands unique in its class, as orderless and unorganized, as irresponsible, earthy and surprising as the characters in it. The finished art of *The Satyricon* seems entirely unpremeditated, like the natural outflow of genius which does not require revision. It has the lightness of a vocal narrative by a good story-teller whose vocabulary is always equal to his sense of life and his sense of humor.

Although *The Satyricon* is by implication a satire, it is not a satire by observable intention. The figure of Trimalchio is actually drawn sympathetically, with the sympathy of deep humor. To Petronius, Trimalchio is preposterous and absurd, but not an object of pity or censure; he is an amusing clown who is a product at once of his nature, his origins, and his environment. His attempts at grandeur, his pretensions to learning and taste, his efforts in the arts are all funny: there is nothing evil or reprehensible about them. He has a childish pride in his achievements and acquisitions (he tells his guests that once he was no higher in station than they are but that he had the stuff in him and thus rose to grandeur on the precept "buy wisely, sell wisely," and under the providence of the three gods, Toil, Luck, and Profit); he brags in season and out, but his heart is comparatively pure; his vulgarity is fabulous but he is the epitome of bourgeois virtues—thrifty, canny, monogamous, grateful to, and dependent upon, his wife, with whom he quarrels like a fish monger in company and alternately berates and extols (one moment he tells his guests in her presence that he took the "sleazy old bitch," the "old rattlesnake," "the wooden dummy" out of a low-down shanty and the chorus of a burlesque show and made a lady out of her; and in the next he tells what a brick she was when he lost all his money in a speculation one time and gave him her jewels and savings so he could get another start); he delights in playing grotesque practical jokes on his guests, but he feeds them well in a spirit that is benevolently democratic; and there is, after all, something both wistful and comic about his aspirations.

Trimalchio's banquet is no doubt a burlesque of the Lucullan feasts popular among the Roman profiteers of the time, in which each tried to outdo the other in rarity of delicacies, variety and ingenuity of entertainment, extravagance in display and sottishness in gobbling and guzzling. The trend of the conversation at Trimalchio's dinner table is almost startlingly modern in vocabulary and quality—so like the conversation in the home of a very rich American who prides himself on his acquaintance with, and encouragement of, the arts hardly less than on his ability to call the turns in the market. Petronius reproduces with faithful exactitude the various idioms and emphases, the jargon and the shop-talk of the representatives of various trades and professions at the feast.

The banquet enables Petronius to include in his novel anecdotes, parodies of the poetry of Lucan (author of the *Pharsalia* and poet laureate at the court of Nero) and of the light verse of the time, the first werewolf story in literature, examples of poor jokes and epigrams such as a person like Trimalchio would indulge in, astrological nonsense, Babbittry in literary, historical and mythological lore (all of it mixed-up, ignorant and sophomoric), and talk of wine, food and money.

The third section of the book is by way of contrast to the second. Here Encolpius meets the aged and indigent poet, Eumolpus, who was once a tutor in Pergamum. The old fellow is threadbare and seedy and as much on the lookout for a free meal as Encolpius, but he still has a regard for the things of the mind and spirit. At the dinner

Encolpius, Ascyltus and the other guests are represented as becoming progressively bored by the efforts of Trimalchio to be entertaining, and, while trying to appear to enjoy Trimalchio's verses and conversation (that they might be invited again), getting drunker and drunker out of the sheer mental fatigue of listening.

When Encolpius meets Eumolpus in an art gallery (the first description of an art gallery in literature) the conversation is at once on a higher level, the stories have point, and the poetry is excellent. In this section we have the famous Milesian tale, *The Matron of Ephesus* (one of the earliest, best and most imitated of short stories), some really excellent poetry in *The Siege of Troy* and the *Civil War*, and some discussions of art and literature that have value. Some commentators, observing that the poems in this section are about as good as any in Latin literature although put into the mouth of the down-at-the-heel Eumolpus, have been puzzled by them, not knowing whether to take them seriously or as parodies. The point, however, is that Petronius is showing by contrast with the shoddy verses of the middle section, the difference between the pretense of wealthy vulgarians to literary taste and talent and the real thing, and incidentally showing to the world that he, Petronius, can write excellent poetry as well as excellent prose.

Although Encolpius makes fun of Eumolpus' addiction to poetry, he nevertheless respects the old fellow's genius. In one scene, at the most terrifying moment of a shipwreck, Eumolpus is depicted as discovered in the captain's cabin piling up verses on a huge piece of parchment, nor will he allow himself to be dragged away to safety without kicking and screaming, "Let me finish my poem! It is nearly finished!" Although Petronius permits the narrator to call Eumolpus a lunatic, he knows that to a real poet the completion of a poem when the frenzy is on is more important than anything else. Later on Eumolpus scores those amateur versifiers who imagine that writing poetry is easy and who write poetry "in their spare time"; he says that only fools believe that when they have written a line that scans they have written poetry; and then he gives some excellent pointers on what constitutes a good poem.

In the third and last section the fight of Encolpius and Ascyltus for the possession of Giton continues. Encolpius has kidnaped Giton and Ascyltus in searching wildly for him when Encolpius, Eumolpus and Giton take refuge on shipboard, whereon Encolpius' anxiety and jealousy are increased because he now finds he has two rivals for Giton's affections, Eumolpus and Tryphæna, the wife of the captain. Much of this section has been lost and what we have of the original text is badly mutilated. It appears that in the lost portions of the manuscript there were reasons why Encolpius wished to avoid Tryphæna and her husband, Lichas. He, Eumolpus and Giton thereupon get their heads shaved to disguise themselves as slaves. A passenger sees them at the barber's and reports this to the captain, for it was considered bad luck for anybody aboard ship to have his hair cut on a voyage.

The captain is in terror and orders his sailors to give them forty stripes apiece with the cat-o'-nine-tails to propitiate the deity with their blood. A burlesque forensic bout follows between Eumolpus and Lichas, in which Eumolpus is counsel for the defense. The debate enlists partisans on both sides and soon all aboard ship are in a fight. A truce is declared through the good offices of Tryphæna, a pact is signed between Encolpius and Lichas, and then Lichas incredibly bursts into a recital of execrable verses.

With harmony restored Eumolpus relates the story of the matron of Ephesus and all goes well until a storm comes up and the ship is wrecked. Lichas perishes in the waves and Encolpius, who has reached land with his companions, on seeing the body of the captain washed upon the shore, delivers himself of an affecting soliloquy:

Where now is your angry heart? Where now your untamed spirit? Verily, you are a prey to fishes and wild beasts; but yesterday you were boasting of your high authority; today you are a ship-wrecked sailor; and of your lordly ship, not even one timber remains.

Go then, poor mortals! Fill your souls with soaring plans. Go, in the pride of your prudence, and lay out for a thousand years the wealth you stole by trickery! Verily, this man only yesterday counted up his wealth; verily he even fixed the very day when he would land at home again. Ye gods and goddesses, how far from his goal he lies! It is not only the seas that play these tricks on men. One man is ruined in the pride of his arms;

another while he is sacrificing to the gods is buried in the ruins of his home; another is flung headlong from his coach and breathes his last. Food chokes the greedy; moderation the abstemious. Add up the sum exactly and you find shipwreck everywhere.

The vagabonds go next to Crotona, a city described as being without art or industry, the whole population being divided between legacy hunters and legacy leavers. A peasant tells them that in Crotona "No one brings up children, for the reason that no one who has heirs is invited to dinner or admitted to the games; such a one is deprived of all enjoyment and must lurk with the rabble. On the other hand those who have never married a wife, or those who have no near relatives, attain to the very highest honors; in other words they are the only ones considered soldierly, or the bravest of the brave, or even good. You will see a town which resembles the fields in time of pestilence, in which there is nothing but carcasses to be torn at and carrion crows tearing at them." [3]

Encolpius is for avoiding the city but Eumolpus has a grandiose idea. He puts it into effect. He poses as a millionaire who has been shipwrecked with his slaves; he constantly refers to his estates, his silver and gold, complains of the food and in every way draws the hopes and expectations of the legacy-hunters of Crotona to him. They heap gifts upon him, invite him to sumptuous dinners and do everything to earn his gratitude. Eumolpus makes out

[3] Firebaugh's translation.

his elaborate will with a strange codicil and reads it, bringing more wealth in gifts to him. Meanwhile Encolpius has a fantastic amorous encounter with a rich woman called Circe and with a younger woman named Chrysis. The legacy-hunters become impatient because Eumolpus lingers on so long and finally begin to lose faith in his promises. They resolve to seize Eumolpus, Encolpius and Giton and punish them for having lived so long at the public expense. Encolpius and Giton take to the road in fright, leaving Eumolpus to his fate. They learn that Eumolpus is put to death in "the Massilian manner." (Whenever the Massilians were ravaged by the plague one of the poor would offer himself as a scapegoat, to be fed for a whole year upon choice food at public expense, then "loaded with imprecations so that he might take to himself the evils from which the city suffered" he was hurled from a cliff.)

Thus ends one of the magnificent sports (in biological terminology) of literature. Whether or not there was more of the narrative we do not know. A delighted posterity of at least a few dozen persons may some day greet the appearance of the complete manuscript of *The Satyricon,* removed perhaps, like the precious fragments of Sappho and Menander, from a mummy case where it has served for centuries as wadding. Or perhaps some carnal monk, risking his soul under the temptations of the Devil, may have hidden away intact, for his own secret delectation, this realistic revelation of life under the decadence of the

Roman empire, and maybe the monk's sin will gratify the scholarly and the curious and lovers of good writing at some distant date.

Meanwhile what we have of *The Satyricon* is a precious possession. It is entertainment pure and simple, but of the most sophisticated kind, far removed from messages, morals and homilies. There is much in it to offend the prudish; but it is nowhere a provocation to lust, which is a common enough attribute of human beings anyhow and never in much need of provocations. Indeed, Petronius delights to depict the discomfitures of physical love and to smile indulgently upon the acrobatics of the sexually possessed. A sense of the comic never deserts him; and he does but give us an earnest of his seriousness in the reverential attitude he takes toward his work. He is an artist for whose work the judicious might give a dozen Virgils, Ciceros, Senecas and Juvenals. He pictured imperishable traits in human nature in characters who are animated with the authentic breath of life. He was a liberator of the spirit and of the language: he avoided being "literary" and wrote as people talked.

NOTE

The only complete and unabridged translations of *The Satyricon* in English are the one attributed to Oscar Wilde (printed for private circulation in England in 1902; and later printed for subscribers only by Pascal Covici, Chicago, 1927), and the one by W. C. Firebaugh, published for private circulation only, by Boni & Liveright, New York, 1922.

Firebaugh has included the forgeries but has indicated them by brackets. In the so-called Wilde translation the chapters are not numbered and the forgeries are not indicated.

Translations of *Trimalchio's Banquet* only have been made by M. J. Ryan, W. D. Lowe and Harry Thurston Peck.

The first English translation was made by William Burnaby and published in London in 1694. In 1929 a reprint of the Burnaby translation, with a preface by C. K. Scott Moncrieff, was issued in London, but my copy does not indicate the publisher. Burnaby, like many later translators, leaves the franker passages in the Latin original. His is a quaint and interesting version.

The French poet, Laurent Tailhade, translated *The Satyricon* into modern colloquial French, using many words current in the argot of the Parisian underworld, for which he supplied a glossary. My edition is that published in 1922 by Editions de la Sirène. This is a lively and felicitous translation. Previous to the Tailhade translation the standard French version was that of J. N. M. de Guerle, published by Garnier Frères.

The W. K. Kelly translation in the Bohn library is wooden.

The complete text with a translation by M. Heseltine is available in the Loeb Classical Library.

J. M. Mitchell in 1922 published, through George Routledge & Sons, Ltd., London, an excellent if very English, modern version, and from this version I have quoted once. Mitchell, like Firebaugh, supplied extensive notes. Firebaugh also includes Marchena's notes (which, by the way, I translated for Firebaugh, although he neglected to acknowledge this).

Bibliographical references for the above chapter may include: *Jewish Antiquities* and *The Wars of the Jews* by Flavius Josephus, in any translation; Dill's *Roman Society from Nero to Marcus Aurelius* and *Roman Society: The Last Century of the Western Empire;* Gibbon's History of the *Decline and Fall of the Roman Empire; The Annals* of Tacitus; *Lives of the Twelve Cæsars* by Suetonius; Collington's *Etude sur Petrone*, Paris, 1905; Beck's *Age of Petronius,* Cambridge, 1857; Mommsen's *Trimalchios Heimat,* Hermes tr., 1878; Charles Whibley's *Studies in Frankness,* London, 1910; and B. Henderson's *Life and Principate of the Emperor Nero,* London, 1905.

LUCIAN

LUCIAN

*

THE most popular, the most imitated, writer of the Italian Renaissance was not a Greek of the Golden Age of Athenian literature, nor was he a Latin author of the Augustan age, but Lucian of Samosata, a Syrian of Semitic stock who, like Terence, Apuleius and Joseph Conrad, mastered an alien tongue and became one of the finest adornments of a literature which was not native with him.

I believe it is in the cards that Lucian will shortly regain the prestige he enjoyed during the Renaissance and with the Elizabethans. John Jay Chapman recently published a little book on Lucian and Plato, contrasting them to the latter's disadvantage and arguing with considerable point and cogency that Lucian has much more to say to us now than has Plato and that the quality of Lucian's mind is more agreeable to us than Plato's. Charles Whibley in England (or rather more correctly, in Scotland) has done much to revive an interest in Lucian; and

the extraordinarily felicitous translation of Lucian made
by the Fowler brothers for the Oxford University Press,
and the courageous, more complete, hardly less felicitous
and more literal translation, in seven volumes, by Professor A. M. Harmon of Princeton for the Loeb Library
are there to reveal to any one who cares to read them
that Lucian is as modern as Anatole France, James
Branch Cabell, Ring Lardner, H. L. Mencken, and P. G.
Wodehouse, each of whom he at one point or another
resmbles.

In the fifteenth century Fifelfo, Guarino and Poggio
in Italy translated Lucian, and Rudolph Agricola introduced him north of the Alps. "He had more imitators,"
writes Preserved Smith in his biography, *Erasmus,* "than
any other Greek writer. Thomas More, Pirckheimer,
Mosellanus, Ottomar Luscinus and Melanchthon all tried
their hands at versions of his dialogues. His strong influence was reflected in the numerous satires of the age (of
Erasmus), in the *Praise of Folly* and in the works of
Rabelais. . . . He (Erasmus) speaks particularly of Lucian,
the author of the dialogues on the fly, on the parasite, and
on the ass, and of course Erasmus' careful study and translation of this author contributed to his own mastery of
style."

It is obvious that Shakespeare was acquainted with
Lucian: his *Timon of Athens* is derived from Lucian's
Timon, or The Misanthrope, and his plays are studded
with tag-lines and phrases which were either lifted bodily

from Lucian's text (lines like "There is method in his madness") or had already passed from Lucian, in translation, into the phrasal currency of the time. Either Shakespeare knew more Greek than he is credited with learning or he had familiarized himself with Sir Thomas More's version of Lucian or with that of Erasmus or some other translator. Marlowe, Jonson, and Robert Burton reveal their indebtedness to Lucian in page after page, and, indeed, the most famous example of the "mighty line of Marlowe" (the "Was this the face that launched a thousand ships and burnt the topless towers of Ilium?") is almost a word for word translation from Lucian. Dryden, in a later generation, not only drew upon Lucian for material and inspiration but translated some of the *Dialogues* with a wit and vivacity which has never been surpassed.

The verdict of the Dutch critic, Hoogstraten, that Lucian is "not only the greatest genius of his own age, but even of all antiquity," is one which I am enthusiastically inclined to share. Lucian was, in literature, almost a universal genius: he invented a new literary form; his essays on the arts of writing, pantomime, sculpture, and painting are better than Aristotle's or Plato's and unexcelled in modern times; he was one of the greatest parodists that ever lived; he was a rationalist of the caliber of Voltaire in an age when almost no one was rational and an ironic wit of the caliber of Anatole France in an age when credulity was most preposterous; he predicted

aviation and telegraphic communication; he was learned
in the tricks of the conjurors and thaumaturgists and
exposed them on every hand; he satirized the shams of
the philosophers and the rhetoricians; he created characters in his dialogues with a sure genius; and he had a
personal method of expression whereby, with a judiciously
placed phrase, he could contrive at once a provocation to
laughter and an implied comment which illuminated his
whole sane and intelligent understanding of human nature
and conduct.

Lucian, indeed, is the most modern of all writers of
antiquity, more modern even than Horace, because the
range of his interests is wider than Horace's. His skepticism is complete; his feet are on the ground; his mind
is clear, sharp and incisive; and he had learned the crafts-
manship of his art to perfection. Writing five hundred
and fifty years after the great period of Greek literature
and after that literature had degenerated under Alexandrian and Byzantine influences, he, a foreigner, wrote with
classical clarity and limpidity. He was an enemy of sham
and pretense, false art, bogus history, highfalutin oratory,
scheming politicians, hypocritical philosophers, the pagan
priesthood, rhetoricians, the ostentatious rich, vulgar display, and those cringing scholars who are content to abase
their souls for a post in the house of a patron. He runs
the whole gamut of comedy, satire, humor, wit, parody,
and sheer clowning. And behind it all is a fascination
and delight in the spectacle of life. "When I saw all this,"

he says in the character of Menippus, "the life of man came before me under the likeness of a great pageant, arranged and marshalled by Chance, who distributed infinitely varied costumes to the performers."

In Lucian's *Dialogues*, Zeus, the overlord of the Greek Pantheon, is always at once a comic and infinitely human character: he shirks his work whenever he can, gets perplexed and bored by the numerous and contradictory prayers and petitions offered up to him, and from time to time wants to get away from it all.

In one of the *Dialogues of the Gods*, Zeus is all upset. Hera, his wife, thinks it is a love affair that is bothering him. Hera says, "I suppose you have discovered some new Danæ or Semele or Europa whose charms are troubling you; and so you are meditating a transformation into a bull or satyr, or a descent through the roof into your beloved's bosom as a shower of gold; all the symptoms—your groans and your tears and your white face—point to love and nothing else."

Zeus tells her, in effect, that it is not a love affair; he hasn't time for such things now; his business has got him worried. She demands, like any wife, to know whether his name is Zeus or not ("Are you the boss of that outfit or are you not? If you are, let them know you are boss"); but Zeus tells her that a very bad situation has arisen:

"My dear," Zeus says, "a discussion somehow arose yesterday between Timocles the Stoic and Damis the Epicurean; there was a numerous and respectable audience (which particularly annoyed me), and they had an argument on the subject of Providence. Damis questioned the existence of the Gods, and utterly denied their interest in or government of events, while Timocles, good man, did his best to champion our cause. A great crowd gathered round; but no conclusion was reached. They broke up with an understanding that the inquiry should be completed another day; and now they are all agog to see which will win and prove his case. You all see how parlous and precarious is our position, depending on a single mortal. These are the alternatives for us: to be dismissed as mere empty names, or (if Timocles prevails) to enjoy our customary honors."

Hera agrees that the matter is serious; and so Zeus tells Hermes to summon the gods to council. Hermes bawls out: "Here, assemble, all ye Gods; don't waste time, come along, here you are; we are going to have an important meeting."

Zeus: What, Hermes? So bald, so plain, so prosy an announcement—on this momentous occasion?

Hermes: Why, how would you like it done?

Zeus: Some meter, a little poetic sonority, would make the style impressive, and they would be more likely to come.

Hermes says that he is no good at poetry; that whatever he should compose would be sure to have too many feet or not enough. Zeus tells him he can swipe some lines from Homer and change the words around a bit.

Hermes tries to recite his own rôle as conceived by Homer in summoning the gods to council and, like most people trying to sing *The Star Spangled Banner,* he has to put in "tum-tum" for words he has forgotten.

The gods come running pell-mell, all trying to grab the best seats. Zeus tells Hermes to place them in the order of preference—that is, according to the cost of the statuary of them. The Egyptian and barbarian gods and goddesses get the front row because their statues are all of solid gold. The Greek gods, although "they have grace and beauty and artistic workmanship," are all marble or bronze, "and even those are wood inside, harboring whole colonies of mice." Poseidon asks, "Hermes, is it in order that this dog-faced Egyptian person should sit in front of me?" Hermes tells him that of course it is, because the snout-nosed Egyptian deity is a whole gold-mine richer than Poseidon because Lysippus, the sculptor, made the latter of paltry bronze. Aphrodite claims a seat in the first row because Homer had called her "The Golden Aphrodite," and Hermes answers, "Oh, yes, no doubt; *he* called Apollo rich, 'rolling in gold'; but now where will you find Apollo? Somewhere in the third-class seats; his crown has been taken off and his harp pegs stolen by the pirates, you see [referring to the condition of Apollo's statue at the time—B.R.]. So *you* may think yourself lucky with a place above the fourth."

The gods are noisy and chattering, some of them bawling, "What, no ambrosia?" "When do we eat?"

"Here, shares in that victim!" The gang is presently brought to order; but Zeus, who is presiding, has stage-fright and forgets what he wanted to say. He had a speech all prepared but he can't remember a word of it.

Zeus: What do you think? Reel off the exordium in Homer?

Hermes: Which one?

Zeus: Lend me your ears, Gods all and Goddesses.

Hermes: Rubbish! you made quite exhibition enough of yourself in that vein in our cabinet council. However, you might, if you like, drop your metrical fustian, and adapt any one of Demosthenes's Philippics with a few alterations. That is the fashionable method with speakers nowadays.

Zeus: Ah, that is a royal road to eloquence—simplifies matters very much for a man in difficulties.

Hermes: Go ahead then.

Zeus: Men of—Heaven, I presume that you would be willing to pay a great price, if you could know what in the world has occasioned the present summons. Which being so, it is fitting that you should give a ready hearing to my words. Now, whereas the present crisis, Heavenians, may almost be said to lift up a voice and bid us take vigorous hold on opportunity, it seems to me that we are letting it slip from our nerveless grasp. And I wish now (I can't remember any more) to exhibit clearly to you the apprehensions which have led to my summoning you. . . .

After this delicious parody of oratorical rodomontade (true to type now as it was in the days of Lucian and previously) Zeus tells them that the god business is in a bad way. Only yesterday a ship's captain whose ship was driving against a cliff vowed to the gods whole hecatombs if his ship should escape destruction. What the ship's captain actually offered, after the boat had been saved, was "a single cock—an old bird afflicted with catarrh—and half a dozen grains of frankincense." Right after that Zeus heard some philosophers of the "militant variety" arguing on a corner and so he disguised himself as a philosopher by lengthening his beard and elbowed his way through the crowd to hear what they were saying. An Epicurean was denying the existence of the gods and a Stoic was asserting their existence. Zeus could plainly see that the Epicurean was getting the better of the argument. The debate was to continue and if Damis won the goose would be cooked for the Heavenians.

Zeus asks for suggestions. Momus is the first to respond. He is a sardonic and straight-thinking fellow. Momus here is a reflection of Lucian himself. He asks: "What can you expect men to think, when they see all life topsy-turvy—the good neglected, pining in poverty, disease, and slavery; detestable scoundrels honored, rolling in wealth, and ordering their betters about, temple-robbers undetected and unpunished, the innocent constantly crucified and bastinadoed? With this evidence before them, it is only natural they should conclude against our existence. All the more when they hear the oracles saying that some one

The Halys crossed, o'erthrows a mighty realm

but not specifying whether that realm is his own or his enemies'; or again

O sacred Salamis, thou shalt slay
Full many a mother's son.

The Greeks were mothers' sons as well as the Persians, I suppose. Or again, when they hear the ballads about our loves, our wounds, captivities, thraldoms, quarrels, and endless vicissitudes (mark you, we claim all the while to be blissful and serene), are they not justified in ridiculing and belittling us?"

Momus goes on to say that all the gods do is sit and see that there are plenty of sacrifices on the altars. Then Zeus resorts to the old dodge of saying that any one can criticize destructively; that what is needed is constructive criticism, "a statesman suggesting a better course." Poseidon suggests that Zeus hurl a thunderbolt; but Zeus replies that is no way to settle an argument; that if you destroy your adversary beforehand, he dies unvanquished, and leaves his argument behind him still debatable and undecided. Apollo says that Timocles is timid, stammers, loses the thread of his argument and is given to a flowery language which is confused and unintelligible. He says that what is needed is lucidity. Momus promptly tells Apollo that he is a fine one to talk about lucidity, inasmuch as Apollo's oracles are so ambiguous that a second prophet is required to figure out what they mean. Hercules suggests that if things begin to go bad with Timocles in the argument he might "give the portico a shake and bring it down on Damis." But Zeus says that is a shocking suggestion—to kill all those people for "one man's wickedness."

At last the argument between Timocles and Damis gets under way. Timocles resorts to invective; Damis is cool and courteous. Zeus comments to the gods, "At this game ours is much the better man—louder-voiced, rougher tempered. Good, Timocles; stick to invective; that is your strong point; once you get off that, he will hook and hold you up like a fish." In the argument of Damis, Lucian foreshadows the Darwinian theory; gives a résumé of the various forms of religious worship of the times; and develops a concise theory of social relationships. Timocles never gets an effective idea and so continues to call his opponent a "scoundrel, thief, body-snatcher, well-whipped scum," and to yell at Damis, "You strangled your own brother, you live in fornication, you debauch the young, you unabashed lecher!"

Damis makes off with a laugh, with Timocles after him hurling imprecations and throwing a crockery pot at Damis' head. The gods are relieved; they have had a narrow escape. But Hermes reminds them that if even a few of those in the audience were "infected" by Damis' reasoning, there remain plenty of Greeks who side with Timocles, "the body and dregs of the people, and the barbarians to a man."

I have given this dialogue almost in toto because it contains so many of the qualities of Lucian's genius. He is an inveterate rationalist and is therefore an enemy of all superstition; he makes the gods ridiculous simply by viewing in a comic light the attributes and actions related of them by the poets; he parodies the empty eloquence of the orators and the oracles of the soothsayers; he gives us an excellent example of a debate between an Epicurean and a Stoic philosopher; and he displays his knack at supplying the opposite image and in using the lively colloquialism. (At one point, Zeus, leaning over a cloud and anxiously following the debate, says to the other gods: "Our man is a goner; he is frightened and trembles; he is going to throw up the sponge, I am certain of it.") He shows us the time-worn method of dealing with an independent thinker bearing a new idea; and that is to appeal to the emotional prejudices of the mob, by accusing the opponent of impiety, immorality, corruption of the young, and enmity toward the state. In our day it suffices for one to wrap the flag around oneself metaphorically, denounce those seeking reforms as "Reds," and declare that the Soviet government advocates "free love," to set the mob by the ear. (That phrase, "to set by the ear," by the way, was first used in literature by Lucian.)

LUCIAN's style is so individual that it comes through to the English reader even in the most infelicitous translations. In good translations, such as those of Dryden, the Fowler brothers, and Harmon, he reads like a contemporary. He is subtler than Bernard Shaw and he has a genius for the finer shades of characterization, a genius Shaw does not possess. He had an eye and ear for the gypsy phrase; he knew the charm of introducing the unexpected image or the surprising turn of thought; he was master of all the tricks of rhetoric and discarded all of the commonplace ones in favor of tricks of his own, tricks which were not really tricks but the natural expression of a highly original mind.

Lucian was exceedingly popular in his own time; but some aspects of his popularity distressed him. He was praised, but for the wrong things. In the *Zeuxis and Atiochus* he tells us that he was walking home after delivering a lecture and that a number of his audience came up to him and introduced themselves and walked along with him, with such laudatory exclamations that he was "reduced to blushing between the praising and the thing praised. Their chief point was that the substance of my work was so fresh, so crammed with novelty."

This did not please him, for, as a serious artist, he objected to being thought of simply as creator of paradoxes. He had once said that "there is no great art without some strangeness in it," but he had also written "in my eyes strangeness without beauty has no merit . . . and I should deserve to be torn to pieces by sixteen vultures if I thought that a work of art could be distinguished by novelty alone." Therefore:

These commendations, to be quite frank, were very far from gratifying to me; when at length they left me to myself, my reflections took this course:—So the only attraction in my work is that it is unusual, and does not follow the beaten track; good vocabulary, orthodox composition, insight, subtlety, Attic grace, general constructive skill—these may for aught I know be completely wanting; else indeed they would hardly have left them unnoticed, and approved my method only as new and startling. Fool that I was, I did indeed guess, when they jumped up to applaud, that novelty was part of the attraction; I knew that Homer spoke truly when he said there is favour for the new song; but I did not see that novelty was to have so vast a share—the whole, indeed—of the credit; I thought it gave a sort of adventitious charm, and contributed its part to the success, but that the real object of commendation—what extracted the cheers—was those other qualities. Why, I have been absurdly self-satisfied, and come very near believing them when they called me the one and only real Greek, and such nonsense. But behold, my gold is turned to ashes; my fame, after all, is little different from that enjoyed by a conjuror.

Lucian was of Semitic stock and because of the likeness of his wit to that of Heinrich Heine, Whibley has suggested that Lucian may have had Jewish blood in his veins. At one time I supported this suggestion in an essay in which I attempted to point out the differences between Greek irony and Jewish irony. But a very important objection to this supposition arises when I recall that Lucian tells us he was apprenticed in boyhood to his maternal uncle, who was a statuary or sculptor. In Lucian's time, Jewish law prohibited the making of images of any sort; and as intermarriage with other races was also forbidden by Jewish law it is extremely unlikely that, if there was a sculptor in Lucian's family, any member of that family was of the Jewish faith. Moreover, Lucian tells us that in his youth he offered a lock of hair to a Syrian goddess; so it is probable that he was brought up in the worship of Astarte.

We have no information as to the exact date of Lucian's birth. Evidence based upon what he tells us about himself seems to place his birth about 125 A.D., and his death about the year 200. He was born in Samosata, in Syria, of parents who were in such humble circumstances that after he had finished his primary schooling he was obliged to seek a trade or profession, to which end he was apprenticed to his uncle. When he was in school, he tells us in *The Vision,* he used to scrape off the wax from his writing tablets and work it into the shapes of cows, horses, and men and women—a practice which caused him frequently to be thrashed by his schoolmasters but which indicated to his father wherein his talents lay.

On the first day of his apprenticeship, however, he had the bad luck to break a valuable piece of marble. His uncle had given him a chisel and had told him to "give a gentle touch to a plaque lying on the bench." He brought the chisel down too hard and the plaque broke; whereupon his uncle flew into a rage and beat him with a stick. He ran home, howling, and showed his mother his bruises, telling her also that his uncle was envious of him and afraid he would become the better sculptor. His mother took his part and upbraided her brother. That night, Lucian tells us, he had a dream in which two women took hold of his hands; one was named Statuary and the other was named Culture. Each argued her own qualities and predicted fame for him if he should follow her. He deemed that Culture put up the better argument, and next day decided to dedicate himself to her service. (The matter of the dream is probably a fiction; but the implication is true to what happened.)

Although Lucian was brought up to speak the Syrian dialect of Aramaic, Greek was the lingua franca of the Near East in his time, and it is probable he was taught Greek in school. He tells us that even before he set his mind to the task of becoming a rhetorician, he had some knowledge of Greek, but that even after long residence in Greece he still spoke with the accent of a barbarian.

Just how he acquired the art of rhetoric, he does not tell us; but one thing is certain, and that is that he was extraordinarily successful at it. It appears that he was an omnivorous reader, and he had a sure instinct for the best of classical Greek expression. He brought to the study of Greek a rare critical faculty which enabled him to perceive faults and absurdities in the work of the most renowned of Greek writers. He had very little respect for Plato, no respect at all for Hesiod; he ridiculed the extravagances of the Greek historians; and he had a sharp eye for evidences of cant and stupidity in the dramatists.

It is instructive to observe that he was untouched by the Alexandrian vices of the decadence of Greek literature (*i.e.*, the vices of ornament, pedantry and eccentric invention), and that he *never quotes a Latin author*. His contempt for that (for the most part) disingenuous and hypocritical literature was profound: in the *Nigrinus* he says that only once in his life does your thoroughbred Roman say what he means—when he is making out his will—"and this occasion comes too late for him to enjoy credit for it."

His greatest financial success seems to have been as a rhetorician in Rome—although he was a conspicuous success in Ionia, Greece, Italy and Gaul—but this does not prevent him from holding the Roman way of life in the utmost distaste. He contrasts Athenian liberty and unpretentiousness in living with the sad spectacle of the vicious Roman economy whereby a large proportion of the populace were even worse than slaves because they had no security beyond the day, whereas the upper-crust of speculators and of men in favor with the emperor lived lives of gluttony, intemperance and display, sleeping throughout the day and giving themselves over to swinish orgies in the night.

There was, in Lucian, a streak of that quality we call puritanism. Whether he followed his own ideals or not we do not know; but insobriety, the brutal gratification of lust, indecency of any sort he ranked among the sins he deplored the most—the sins of avarice, perjury, cozenage, vulgar display, cruelty, usury, charlatanry, pedantry and pretense.

The contempt Lucian had for Roman society and for the dissembling literature produced in that society is so magnificent that it may be well to recall some of the phases and constituents of that anti-social hegemony. And we should remark, in passing, that it is high evidence of Lucian's character that he never permitted himself by emolument or fame to be persuaded into even a feigned admiration for the plunderbund that was Rome. He did not even sharpen his satire against the easy butt of Roman vice, as so many Romans hitherto had done. To do this was much too easy for the conscientious artist that he was. What he did do, with a subtlety of understatement that is absolutely astounding, was to single out for attack the most pretentious prig among the deified Cæsars—Marcus Aurelius—and to let his shaft go when the sainted Marcus was still in power and when Lucian himself was an alien, subject to Roman rule.

Gibbon almost alone among classical historians was never quite taken in by the legend of saintliness that surrounded the name of Marcus Aurelius, and even Gibbon labors his irony in his remarks upon that personage to a degree which makes the import of his sentiments rather difficult to determine. Marcus Aurelius, as you perhaps remember, if you have been unfortunate enough to plow through his venerated and generally unread *Meditations,*

begins his immortal work by enumerating his virtues and
the means whereby he attained them. Articulately he was
an animated wall-motto of the most sentimental type. In
reality he appears not only to have been one of the most
incompetent [1] of many very incompetent Roman emperors,
but also a sullen, sanctimonious and superstitious ruler
who did not hesitate to order pogroms against the Jews and
Christians or to order the slaughter of whole tribes of independent, barbarian folk who refused to pay him tribute.

[1] In saying this I find myself obliged to follow closely the text of
Dion Cassius, Herodian, the anonymous author of the life of Marcus
Aurelius in the *Scriptores Historiæ Augustæ*, and to partake more imper-
fectly of the imperfect sympathy Gibbon retained toward Marcus Aurelius.
The earlier historians, who dedicated their works to Roman princes who
were presumptive heirs to the throne, found so much evil in the characters
no less than in the deeds of the Cæsars, that it was with relief they came
upon the careers of Antoninus Pius, Marcus Aurelius, Trajan and Hadrian.
The first two Antonines were pious, ascetic in temperament, moderate in
temper; whereupon their historians are given to generalities about them
such as saying, "They performed many good deeds, modified the laws,
and took compassion upon the poor, and gave to their subjects examples
of Stoic austerity"—and then they go on to enumerate specific actions
which show that the Antonines were, as emperors, as grasping and as
predatory as their predecessors and, in some cases, even more so. We learn,
for instance, how thoughtful it was of Marcus Aurelius to order that
mats should be spread under trapeze performers at the circus when he
witnessed the death of one of these performers who had fallen to the
ground and broken his neck (from which edict, our ancient historian
informs us, all circuses now have nets under the trapeze performers). This
was thoughtful. But at the same time Marcus Aurelius was waging wars
of plunder and subjection in northern Europe and Asia Minor to supply
the upper crust of Roman society, who earned nothing, with luxuries
and to give "bread and circuses" to an enormous population of virtual
slaves who also produced nothing in real wealth. The Roman hegemony
was viciously constituted from the beginning, and not even the saintliest
of saints, if he were elevated to dictatorial supremacy in the empire,
could forfend the accusations that may legitimately be made against him;
for, as emperor, he was constrained to exact from the work of the many
to sustain the indolence and depravity of the few.

Generations of male historians have maligned his wife, Faustina, while contributing to the apotheosis of Marcus Aurelius. Faustina, so the gossip goes, strayed from the conjugal embraces of her platitudinous husband (as what woman of spirit would not?) and sought felicity in a society less odorous of tuberoses and calla lilies. (May some of my descendants—female preferably—consult the records assiduously and rehabilitate the character of Faustina.) It is amusing, if impious, to recall that, whereas there were many Christian Fathers and many saintly men since then who have pointed to the *Meditations* of Marcus Aurelius as a divine ordinance that God was working His will even among the pagans and teaching them to inscribe sentiments similar to the Scriptures, Marcus Aurelius himself was, while composing his *Meditations,* giving out orders for the slaughter of Christians as often as he had a séance with the imperial astrologer.

The resolution of Christian apologists to affirm the close affinity of Marcus Aurelius with Jesus at the same time Marcus Aurelius was very intent upon exterminating the Christians is one of those paradoxes that would seem insuperable if one did not read the daily newspapers and learn that juries and men in the mass venerate extravagantly the men who have gypped them, hoping, it would seem, that, with the proper posits of circumstance, they themselves will be the recipients of those luxurious usufructs they have seen conferred upon others.

In *Alexander, the Oracle Monger,* an exposé of the

conduct and methods of one of the numerous charlatans
of the period, Lucian relates that when Marcus Aurelius
was about to begin his war against the Macromanni and
Quadi he called in Alexander for advice as to how to
proceed in order to terminate his venture successfully.
By the tone of Lucian's sentences, although they are
couched in subdued irony, we are left in no doubt that
Lucian thought that any emperor who should call into
consultation such an impostor as Alexander for advice on
the eve of a military campaign was an imbecile; but
Lucian's recital of the preposterous requirements of the
oracle and of its fatal issue to the Roman army shows
Lucian's keen appreciation of the ludicrous, especially
when it involved the antics of an emperor destined before
his demise solemnly to be proclaimed a living god by the
senate and people of Rome.

"The oracle," Lucian writes, "required that two lions
should be flung alive into the Danube, with quantities of
sacred herbs and magnificent sacrifices. I had better give
the words:

> To rolling Ister, swoln with Heaven's rain,
> Of Cybelean thralls, those mountain beasts,
> Fling ye a pair; therewith all flowers and herbs
> Of savour sweet that Indian air doth breed.
> Hence victory, and fame, and lovely peace.

These directions were precisely followed; the lions swam
across to the enemy's bank, where they were clubbed to
death by the barbarians, who took them for dogs or a

new kind of wolves; and our forces immediately thereafter met with a severe defeat, losing some twenty thousand men in one engagement."

Marcus Aurelius, indeed, was very superstitious and
quaintly gullible. When Faustina confessed to him that
she was in love with a gladiator, he consulted Chaldean
oracle mongers as to what he should do. They told him
"that the gladiator should be killed and that Faustina
should bathe in his blood and thus couch with her husband.
When this was done, the passion was indeed allayed, but
their son, Commodus, was born a gladiator, not really a
prince; for afterwards as emperor he fought almost a
thousand gladiatorial bouts before the eyes of the
people." [2]

Lucius Verus, until his death, shared the throne with
his adoptive brother, Marcus Aurelius. The circumstances
surrounding Verus' death were mysterious. Some historians
have hinted that he was murdered by Marcus Aurelius
or at his request. In the main, however, historians have
been awed by the smug complacency of the *Meditations*,
and have given Lucius Verus as well as Faustina an evil
character. Julius Capitolinus in his biography of Lucius
Verus [3] set the standard in this denigration when he
wrote:

"When he (Lucius Verus) set out for Syria, however,

[2] *The Scriptores Historiæ Augustæ*, Vol. I, page 179, Loeb Classical
Library edition, edited and translated by David Magie.
[3] *Scriptores Historiæ Augustæ*, Vol. I, page 215, Loeb Classical
Library.

his name was smirched not only by the licence of an un-
bridled life, but also by adulteries and by love-affairs with
young men. Besides, he is said to have been so depraved as
to install a cook-shop in his home after he returned from
Syria, and to repair thither after Marcus' banquets and
have all manner of foul persons serve him. It is said, moreover, that he used to dice the whole night through, after
he had taken up that vice in Syria, and that he so rivalled
Caligula, Nero, and Vitellius in their vices as to wander
about at night through taverns and brothels with only a
common travelling-cap for a head-covering, revel with
various rowdies, and engage in brawls, concealing his
identity the while."

I quote this passage first, because Gibbon repeats the
slander regarding Lucius Verus' perversion (only to remark in a footnote that of the first fifteen emperors
Claudius was "the only one whose taste in love was entirely correct," and later, Vol. I, Chapter 3, page 79, to
describe Claudius with the single adjective "stupid");
second, to show that Julius Capitolinus was entirely un-
reliable; and third, to lead up to Lucian's verdict concerning Lucius Verus.

Julius Capitolinus wrote during the reigns of Dio-
cletian and Constantine the Great, that is to say about
150 years after Lucius Verus was coemperor with Marcus
Aurelius and governor over Syria. Lucian, on the other
hand, was living in Syria at the very time Lucius Verus
was there. Lucian, as I have pointed out before, had a

very low opinion of the Romans and the Roman way of life; he was fastidious in conduct and he had a great loathing of homosexuality. If Lucius Verus had been anything like the sort of person he is described by Julius Capitolinus, Lucian would have seared him with satire.

Now Lucian knew Lucius Verus. What is more, he knew the emperor's mistress, Panthea, and he addressed to her one of the noblest panegyrics in literature, *A Portrait Study*. She was an Ionian woman, from Smyrna; she was brilliant and beautiful, modest and virtuous. Her reply to Lucian's tribute to her, in which she reproved him for irreverent extravagance in likening her to Hera and Aphrodite, is a model of gentle wisdom and tact. She begins by saying, "Your pages are most kind and complimentary, I am sure. No one would have so overpraised me who had not felt kindly toward me. But if you would know my real feeling, here it is. I never do much like the complaisant; they always strike me as insincere and wanting in frankness." Then, among other things, she said of his likening her to Hera and Aphrodite: "Such comparisons are far too high for me or indeed for any of womankind. Why, I would not have you put me on a level with women of the Heroic Age, with a Penelope, an Arete, a Theano; how much less with the chief of the Goddesses. Where the Gods are concerned, I am very apprehensive and timid. I fear that to accept a panegyric like this would be to make a Cassiopeia of myself; though indeed *she* only challenged the Nereids, and stopped short of Hera and Aphrodite."

Lucian, in enumerating Panthea's virtues, says, "You are aware that gentleness, humanity, magnanimity, modesty, culture, are things that I prize more than beauty"; he says that she "is far removed from all thought of arrogance and ostentation. . . . Every man is her equal; her greeting, her smile are for all who approach her," and she is courteous, benevolent and constant in her love.

Now, the sort of man who enjoyed the companionship of a woman like Panthea, whom Lucian likens to the wife of King Abradatas of Susa in praise of whose loyalty Xenophon was so eloquent, could not, in the very nature of things, be the sort of man described by Julius Capitolinus and the historians who repeated his calumnies. It is necessary to be on guard in reading the work of Latin historians, Tacitus included, for most of them have the minds of the worst species of tabloid newspaper editors, centered upon sensationalism. As evidence of this, one has only to recall that precisely the same story as Julius Capitolinus relates above concerning Lucius Verus is told about Nero in Tacitus' *Annals,* and about Otho and Commodius by Suetonius.

Lucian was the implacable enemy of all oracle mongers, diviners, faith "healers," and other charlatans who preyed upon the ignorant and superstitious (a class that embraced the bulk of the population of the Roman empire from the emperor down). Nor was his enmity expressed in mere vituperation of quacks and quackery: he chose to expose the most celebrated oracle monger of his time, the diviner in whose forecasts Marcus Aurelius had as much faith as the late J. P. Morgan had in the late Evangeline Adams,—Alexander of Abonutichus. And when Lucian went about the business of exposing anybody he did it with the utmost thoroughness. He not only learned everything about him; he learned the secret of every trick the impostor performed. Indeed, from Lucian one might compile a manual of imposture that, once mastered by a clever and unscrupulous man, would make him the richest fraud in Los Angeles.

Lucian begins by describing Alexander's appearance: "He was a handsome man, with a real touch of divinity about him, white-skinned, moderately bearded; he wore besides his own hair artificial additions which matched it so cunningly that they were not generally detected. His eyes were piercing and suggested inspiration, his voice was sweet and sonorous." Moreover: "In understanding, resource, acuteness, he was far above other men; curiosity, receptiveness, memory, scientific ability—all these were his in overflowing measure." Yet, with all these qualifications, which should have brought Alexander legitimate rewards in life, he had in him a streak of perversity similar to that of the born crook of our times who prefers to promote a fake stock deal with the risk of making nothing and going to the penitentiary besides than to expend a like amount of energy in a legitimate enterprise in which his profit is certain. "You are to set your imagination to work," writes Lucian, "and conceive a temperament curiously compounded of falsehood, trickery, perjury, cunning; it is versatile, audacious, adventurous, yet dogged in execution; it is plausible enough to inspire confidence; it can assume the mask of virtue and seem to eschew what it most desires."

In his youth Alexander apprenticed himself to "one of those charlatans who deal in magic and incantations; they will smooth your course of love, confound your enemies, find your treasure, or secure you an inheritance." This charlatan was an associate of Apollonius of Tyana and "acquainted with all his heroics." When Alexander's instructor died he formed a partnership with "a Byzantine chronicler of the strolling competitive order, a man of still worse character than himself, called, I believe, Cocconas. The pair went about living on occult pretensions, shearing 'fat-heads,' as they describe ordinary people in the native Magian lingo. Among these they got hold of a rich Macedonian woman; her youth was past, but not her desire for admiration."

With the money they had swindled from the foolish old female, they went to Macedonia where there is a "breed of large serpents, so tame and gentle that women make pets of them, children take them to bed, they will let you tread on them, have no objection to being squeezed, and will draw milk from the breasts like infants. To these facts (Lucian, ever the skeptic, here puts in an aside) is probably to be referred the common story about Olympias when she was with child of Alexander; it was doubtless one of these that was her bed-fellow. Well, the two saw these creatures, and bought the finest they could get for a few pence.

"And from this point, as Thucydides might say, the war takes it beginning. These ambitious scoundrels were quite devoid of scruples, and they had now joined forces; it could not escape their penetration that human life is under the absolute dominion of two mighty principles, fear and hope, and that any one who can make these serve his ends may be sure of a rapid fortune. They realized that, whether a man is most swayed by the one or the other, what he must most depend upon and desire is a knowledge of futurity. So were to be explained the ancient wealth and fame of Delphi, Delos, Clarus, Branchidæ; it was at the bidding of the two tyrants aforesaid that men thronged the temples, longed for foreknowledge, and to attain it sacrificed their hecatombs or dedicated their golden ingots. All this they turned over and debated, and it issued in the resolve to establish an oracle. If it were successful, they looked for immediate wealth and prosperity; the result surpassed their most sanguine expectations."

Alexander was audacious; he conceived the daring but brilliant plan of moving the scene of his operations to his native Abonutichus, where he meant to have his snake accepted as a god and a temple dedicated to him. This seemed like madness to his partner, but Alexander said that the scheme he had in mind required congenial soil to give it a start and that the population of Abonutichus was made up almost entirely of well-to-do "fatheads."

In the temple of Apollo at Chalcedon Alexander first took the precaution of burying some brazen tablets on which was the statement that very shortly Asclepius with his father Apollo would come to reside in Abonutichus. Then Alexander arranged that the tablets should be discovered. The news flew through all Bithynia and Pontus and, of course, was received with the wildest excitement at Abonutichus. "The people of that place at once resolved to raise a temple, and lost no time in digging the foundations."

Cocconas remained in Chalcedon composing and "discovering" oracles and Sibylline prophecies announcing the advent of Alexander in Abonutichus as the city's protector, and proclaiming him a descendant of Perseus. Meanwhile Alexander had let his hair grow and wore it in long curls; he wore a white doublet with purple stripes and carried a scimitar like Perseus. On his arrival in his native city he affected madness and foamed at the mouth, "a manifestation," observes Lucian, "easily produced by chewing the herb soap-wort, used by dyers; but it brought him reverence and awe." He had manufactured a serpent's head with a human expression out of painted linen, and with a contrivance whereby the mouth could be opened and shut and a forked tongue shoot in and out. This he kept in readiness. Then one night he went to the temple, the foundations of which were still being dug, and deposited in the water that had gathered there a new-born reptile concealed in a goose-egg he had blown.

"Early next morning he rushed into the market-place, naked except for a gold-spangled loin cloth" and climbing upon a platform announced the advent of the God. Great crowds gathered; he delivered a harangue; uttered some unintelligible sounds; and set off at a run for the future temple, the crowd following him. On arriving there, "he got down into the water, chanted in a low voice hymns to Asclepius and Apollo, and invited the God to come, a welcome guest, to the city. He next demanded a bowl, and when this was handed to him, had no difficulty in putting it down at the right place and scooping up, besides water and mud, the egg in which the God had been enclosed; the edges of the aperture had been joined with wax and white lead. He took the egg in his hand and announced that here he held Asclepius.

"The people, who had been sufficiently astonished by the discovery of the egg in the water, were now all eyes for what was to come. He broke it, and received in his hollowed palm the hardly developed reptile; the crowd could see it stirring and winding about his fingers; they raised a shout, hailed the God, blessed the city, and every mouth was full of prayers—for treasure and wealth and

health and all the other good things that he might
give."

Alexander knew the value of suspense and so kept
within doors a few days, while the news spread, until
"the city was filled to overflowing with persons who had
neither brains nor individuality, who bore no resemblance
to men that live by bread, and had only their outward
shape to distinguish them from sheep."

At last Alexander received the multitude in ones and
twos who came for a glimpse of the God. And Alexander
had a miracle for them. Within a brief time the tiny God
had grown into an enormous serpent. Alexander, very im-
posingly attired, sat on a couch. Around his neck was
coiled the body of the snake, with the tail filling his lap
and trailing on the ground; "the patient creature's head
he kept hidden in his armpit, showing the linen head on
one side of his beard exactly as if it belonged to his visible
body." The visitors were permitted to touch the body
of the God but urged to hurry on to the exit to make
room for the rest—to prevent them from taking too close
a look. They gasped at the miracle of the rapid growth
of the God and hurried to spread the news. The exhibition
was free: Alexander wasn't ready to take in money—yet.
"By degrees," writes Lucian, "Bithynia, Galatia, Thrace,
came flocking in, every one who had been present doubtless reporting that he had beheld the birth of a God, and
had touched him after his marvelous development in size
and in expression. Next came pictures and models, bronze

and silver images, and the God acquired a name. By divine command, metrically expressed, he was to be known as Glycon. For Alexander had delivered the line:

Glycon my name, man's light, son's son of Zeus.

"And now at last the object to which all this had led up, the giving of oracular answers to all applicants, could be attained."

Lucian explains with precision and detail just how the oracle worked, how the fat-heads were duped. Each person wrote down his wish or what he wanted to know, fastened the packet with thread, and sealed it with wax. Alexander would receive them, enter the holy place, learn the God's mind upon each, and return the packets with seals intact and the answers attached. He made a killing. But he did not keep the money or put it by for the future. Like any modern manufacturer of face lotion or tooth-paste, he "put it all back into the business," to build it up. He hired "accomplices, attendants, inquiry agents, oracle writers and keepers, amanuenses, seal-forgers, and interpreters." And he advertised, sending agents abroad "to make the shrine known in foreign lands; his prophe-cies, discovery of runaways, conviction of thieves and rob-bers, revelations of hidden treasure, cures of the sick, restoration of the dead to life"—all these were to be ad-vertised. This brought them running and crowding from all points of the compass.

After a while he had some trouble with the Epicu-

reans who tried to expose the imposture. They played
tricks on him and made him ridiculous. But he had a resource ready to hand, like any American patrioteer who
shouts "Red" or "Bolshevik" to down his opponent—and
usually succeeds. Alexander "proclaimed that Pontus was
overrun by atheists and Christians." In Lucian's time
"Atheist" and "Christian" were practically synonymous.
The majority shuddered at the thought that Christians
should be on the increase. The Epicureans were defeated
and Alexander's fame spread.

When his fame reached Italy, Lucian writes, "The
only question was, who should be first; those who did not
come in person sent messages, the powerful and respected
being the keenest of all. First and foremost among these
was Rutilianus; he was in most respects an excellent person, and had filled many high offices in Rome; but he suffered from religious mania, holding the most extraordinary
beliefs on that matter; show him a bit of stone smeared
with unguents or crowned with flowers, and he would in-
continently fall down and worship, and linger about it
praying and asking for blessings. The report about our
oracle nearly induced him to throw up the appointment
he then held, and fly to Abonutichus; he actually did send
messenger upon messenger. His envoys were ignorant servants, easily taken in. They came back having really seen
certain things, relating others which they probably thought
they had seen and heard, and yet others which they deliberately invented to curry favour with their master. So

they inflamed the old man and drove him into confirmed
madness."

Old Rutilianus related the marvels of the Abonutichus
oracle to his friends in court and soon everybody including the emperor was sending questions and wishes to the
charlatan. This suggested to Alexander a magnificent
blackmail scheme. "You know the sort of things that
wealthy and powerful personages would be likely to ask,"
writes Lucian, well, "Opening and reading the packets
which reached him, whenever he came upon an equivocal,
compromising question, he omitted to return the packet;
the sender was under his thumb, bound to his service by
the terrifying recollection of the question he had written
down."

Alexander established a spy system in Rome. His
accomplices learned all they could about people of wealth
or influence, what questions they would be likely to ask,
and hints of their ambitions, so that Alexander could
make the answers good.

Alexander's next step was "the institution of mysteries, with hierophants and torch-bearers complete. The
ceremonies occupied three successive days. On the first,
proclamation was made on the Athenian model to this
effect: 'If there be any atheist or Christian or Epicurean
here spying upon our rites, let him depart in haste; and
let all such as have faith in the God be initiated and all
blessing attend them.' He led the litany with, 'Christians,
avaunt!', and the crowd responded, 'Epicureans, avaunt!'

Then was presented the child-bed of Leto and birth of Apollo, the bride of Coronis, Asclepius born. The second day, the epiphany and nativity of the God Glycon."

Lucian goes on to describe the ritualistic hocus-pocus and religious raree-show put on by Alexander which vastly increased the worshipers of the God Glycon. Very like Los Angeles; and the pitch of religious ecstasy was very like that of a Fundamentalist revival meeting. On one occasion, Lucian relates, an Epicurean was highly imprudent: he heckled Alexander by saying, "It was you who induced So-and-so the Paphlagonian to bring his slaves before the governor of Galatia, charged with the murder of his son who was being educated in Alexandria. Well, the young man is alive, and has come back, to find that the slaves have been cast to the beasts by your machinations."

Alexander was master of the situation. "He directed the company to stone the man on pain of being involved in his impiety and called Epicureans." A distinguished citizen interposed his own body to save the Epicurean. "The man," comments Lucian, "had the narrowest possible escape from being stoned to death—as he richly deserved to be; what business had he to be the only sane man in a crowd of madmen?"

Lucian had watched Alexander's career with keen interest, curiosity, and probably with sadness also. But he had some fun with him. Lucian knew that Alexander wore a wig and one time he asked the God Glycon whether Alexander was bald and "having sealed it publicly with great care, got a night oracle in reply: 'Sarbardalachu malach Attis was not he.' Another time I did up the same question—What was Homer's birthplace—in two packets given under different names. My servant misled him by saying, when asked what he came for, a cure for lung trouble; so the answer to one packet was: 'Cytmide of foam of steed the liniment give.' As for the other packet, he got the information that the sender was inquiring whether the land or sea route to Italy was preferable. So, he answered, without much reference to Homer: 'Fare not by sea; land-travel meets thy need.' I laid a good many traps of this kind for him; here is another. I asked only one question, but wrote outside the packet in the usual form, So-and-so's eight Queries, giving a fictitious name and sending the eight shillings. Satisfied with the payment of the money and the inscription on the packet, he gave me eight answers to my one question. This was, When will Alexander's imposture be detected? The answers contained nothing in heaven or earth, but were all silly and meaningless altogether."

Alexander found out about this and, Lucian relates, "he naturally conceived a violent dislike for me. . . . It is true his dislike was quite justified. On a certain occasion I was passing through Abonutichus, with a spearman and a pikeman whom my friend the governor of Cappadocia had lent me as an escort on my way to the sea. Ascertaining that I was the Lucian he knew of, he sent me a very polite and hospitable invitation. I found him with a numerous company; by good luck I brought my escort. He gave me his hand to kiss according to his usual custom. I took hold of it as if to kiss, but instead bestowed on it a sound bite that must have come near disabling him. The company, who were already offended at my calling him Alexander instead of Prophet, were inclined to throttle and beat me for sacrilege. But he endured the pain like a man, and assured them that he would easily tame me, and illustrate Glycon's greatness in converting his bitterest foes to friends."

Alexander dismissed the company, had a private talk with Lucian and tried to bribe him. Lucian pretended to consider the proposition and went away in a friendly manner. When Lucian was ready to sail, Alexander sent him gifts and offered to find a ship and crew for him, which Lucian accepted. He and his secretary, Xenophon, boarded the ship; he had sent his father and family on to Amastris. "When the passage was half over, I observed the master in tears arguing with his men, which made me very uneasy. It turned out that Alexander's orders were to seize and fling us overboard." But the master lost his nerve and landed Lucian in safety.

Lucian relates some more of the exploits of Alexander and tells of his death and the pompous funeral accorded him. Lucian concludes his exposé with these words, "I think casual readers too may find my essay not unserviceable, since it is not only destructive, but, for men of sense, constructive also."

WE should ponder for a moment the concluding sentence of *Alexander, The Oracle Monger;* for too many commentators, who confuse solemnity with seriousness, have written of Lucian as if he were an irresponsible jester. Even Professor Harmon states in his introduction to his text and translation for the Loeb Classical Library: "Rightly to understand and appreciate Lucian, one must recognize that he was not a philosopher nor even a moralist, but a rhetorician, that his mission in life was not to reform society nor to chastise it, but simply to amuse it."

It is an ancient charge. The earliest I have run across is in Eunapius' introduction to his *Lives of the Philosophers.* Eunapius was born in 346 A.D. and died in 414. He says of Lucian that "he usually took serious pains to raise a laugh"; but he also adds that Lucian "wrote a life of Demonax, a philosopher of his own time, and in that book and a very few others was wholly serious throughout." But to say that Lucian's mission in life was simply to amuse is almost to me like saying that Voltaire, Molière and Swift were merely comedians. No one was more aware than he that satire nearly always fails of its purpose; but so do logic, clear reasoning and attempts like Plato's and Aristotle's to establish a dignified rationale of human behavior and a means to communal peace, prosperity and happiness.

By his attacking all kinds of quackery, imposture, delusion, superstition, imposition, priestly charlatanry and philosophical nonsense Lucian's mission in life was as serious as that of any sage or philosopher. He sought to liberate the mind and spirit from fear and superstition. In an age when not only did the common people believe implicitly in the exploits of the gods as narrated by the poets but such philosophers as Ion, who prided himself on his mastery of Plato's doctrines (so Lucian tells us in *The Lover of Lies,* Loeb Classical Library, Lucian III), believed that chronic rheumatism might be removed by incantation; in an age when such a scoundrel as Alexander could grow rich on the credulity of cobblers and kings; in an age when so many Messiahs appeared that the early Christian writers were kept busy denying the credentials of all but one of them—in such an age Lucian kept a mind serenely skeptical, never disposed to accept anything on faith and always looking for proofs when prodigies were announced to him. If he chuckles or provokes a chuckle it is never until after he has investigated some accepted imbecility, and is turning it into the ridiculous. He did not hold that the countenance of truth was always framed into a frown of severity; he proved that truth may smile. Indeed, it is his almost constant reiteration that the long beard and philosopher's cloak, so prevalent in his time, frequently disguised the cadger, the glutton and the hypocrite, ignorant and indolent, who lived without honest work for the simple reason that the majority of people have an awe of the cloak and a respect for the cloth, whether the wearer is deserving of either or not.

In his minute and relentless study of human nature

and his analysis of human motives (in which, by the way, few writers have ever equaled him), he had had plenty of opportunities for observation. For several years he practiced law at Antioch. He gave it up, he tells us, because of the chicanery of lawyers, the frauds practiced in court, and the selfishness and duplicity of clients who rarely sought equity or justice but to win a suit by whatever means.

After that he engaged in the profession of rhetoric or eloquence. The work included writing speeches and declamations for others to deliver, giving lectures, and teaching grammar and composition. Rhetoricians traveled from city to city in his day and he tells us that he wandered about in Asia, Greece, Italy and Gaul, in which last place he remained until he was about forty years of age, teaching and lecturing so successfully that he was able to retire with considerable wealth.

The reason he was so successful is that he became a thorough master in everything he undertook. Supernally clever, quick to see and learn, he always knew how to master the tools of his trade. I excerpt a passage from *The Purist Purized*, which the Fowler brothers have so deftly transliterated:

Ly. Are you the man whose scent is so keen for a blunder, and who is himself blunder-proof?

Pur. I think I may say so.

Ly. I suppose one must be blunder-proof, to detect the man who is not so?

Pur. Assuredly.

Ly. Do I understand that you are proof?

Pur. How could I call myself educated, if I made blunders at my age?

Ly. Well, shall you be able to detect a culprit, and convict him if he denies it?

Pur. Of course I shall.

Ly. Catch me out, then; I will make one just now.

Pur. Say on.

Ly. Why, the deed is done, and you have missed it.

Pur. You are joking, of course?

Ly. No, upon my honour. The blunder is made, and you none the wiser. Well, try again; but you are not infallible on these sort of things.

Pur. Well?

Ly. Again, the blunder made, and you unconscious.

Pur. How can that be, before you have opened your lips?

Ly. Oh yes, I opened them, and to a blunder; but you never see them. I quite doubt you seeing this one even.

On his return from Gaul, Lucian stayed in Rome for a while and visited the Platonic philosopher, Nigrinus, to whom he dedicated an essay second only to the *Demonax* in showing what virtues he admired in men. Rome, Lucian could not stomach and in praising Nigrinus he made use of the opportunity afforded him, to contrast the life of a man of brains and honor with the average Roman in high places. Money, mostly dishonestly gotten, represented the only standard of achievement in that vulgar city, and tasteless extravagance the only accepted way of advertising one's wealth to the world.

In the course of a description of Roman life, which might well serve as a synopsis of *The Satyricon* of Petronius, Lucian lets fall this observation, "The truth is, gold and ivory and noble mansions are of little avail to their owner, if there is no one to admire them. If we would break the power of the rich, and bring down their pretensions, we must raise up within their borders a stronghold of indifference."

Leaving Rome in disgust, Lucian returned to Athens where he lived the greater part of his life with his wife and children, writing dialogues, parodies, burlesques and essays, and conversing with his intimate friend, Demonax, the philosopher. He gave the philosophical dialogue a new twist and a new form. In *The Double Indictment* he says:

... When I first took him (Dialogue) in hand, he was regarded by the world at large as one whose interminable discussions had soured his temper and exhausted his vitality. His labours entitled him to respect, but he had none of the attractive qualities that could secure him popularity. My first step was to accustom him to walk upon the common ground like the rest of mankind; my next, to make him presentable, by giving him a good bath and teaching him to smile.

In the *Dialogue,* with a raillery less boisterous than that of Aristophanes, a wit more pointed, and a deeper purpose, Lucian exposed the follies and vanities of mankind, and the absurdities and pretensions of the literary men of his day. For only one historian, before or during his time—Thucydides—did he have any respect. In *The Way to Write History* he ridicules the various styles and methods of procedure of the historians, their biases, their propagation of lies, their false perspectives, their setting down absurdities from hearsay, their capacity for inventing the preposterous. Everybody, he says, is writing history—and he therefore undertakes to write one himself in *The True History,* one of the most gorgeously entertaining fantasies in all literature. Characteristically, before he begins it, he relates that when report came that Philip was marching on Corinth, the whole city was thrown into a bustle, "one furbishing his arms, another wheeling stones, a third patching a wall, a fourth strengthening a battlement, every one making himself useful somehow or other. Diogenes having nothing to do—of course no one thought of giving *him* a job—was moved by the sight to gird up his philosopher's cloak and begin rolling his tub-dwelling energetically up and down the Craneum; an acquaintance asked and got the explanation: 'I do not want to be thought the only idler in such a busy multitude; I am rolling my tub to be like the rest.' "

And Lucian says, "I too am reluctant to be the only dumb man in so vociferous a season . . . so I decided to roll my *cask* as best I could."

Lucian's contempt for vainglory is at its mordant best in his account of the life and extinction of the fanatic, Peregrine or Peregrinus, and incidentally this essay more than anything else, except an essay attributed to him but now generally designated as spurious, called *Philopatris,* aroused the animosity of early Christian writers against him. The *Philopatris* shows a much better acquaintance with Christianity than does *The Death of Peregrine*.

Peregrine, whose self-destruction Lucian witnessed with unconcealed satisfaction and even amusement, was a loafer and a humbug who called himself Proteus, and who out of a morbid vanity advertised four years in advance that he was going to cremate himself on a great pyre at the Olympic games. He got himself greatly talked about as a Brahmin adept, giving a fine example of fortitude; he spent weeks digging the pit for the pyre before the games. And then when the time came for him to take the leap, according to Lucian, Peregrine fully thought that the crowd would forcibly dissuade him. No one did, to Lucian's great glee; and so Peregrine postponed the suicide until midnight. Lucian took lodging with a friend two miles and a half from Olympia and went back to see if Peregrine would carry out his announced intention. By this time Peregrine could not postpone his act without humiliation; and, throwing aside his cloak and the club of Hercules he always carried, he stood for a moment, says Lucian, "in scrupulously unclean linen," demanded frankincense to throw upon the fire, turned his face to the South and exclaimed: " 'Gods of my mother, Gods of my father, receive me with favor,' and leapt into the pyre. There was nothing more to be seen, however; the towering mass of flames enveloped him completely."

Peregrine had murdered his father, and so Lucian says, "I saw nothing much in his appealing to his mother's

Gods, but when he included his *father's* in the invocation,
I laughed outright."

Peregrine had begun his career as a wandering
magician and miracle-monger; and in this profession,
according to Lucian, he imposed for a long time upon the
credulity of the Christians while he was still being hunted
for parricide. It is quite certain that the Christians did
not take Peregrine for a god, as Lucian says, but I see no
reason to doubt the account as a whole. I shall quote the
passage as showing the impression Lucian had of the
Christians in 169 A.D.:

It was now that he came across the priests and scribes
of the Christians, in Palestine, and picked up their queer creed.
I can tell you, he pretty soon convinced them of his superiority;
prophet, elder, ruler of the Synagogue—he was everything at
once; expounded their books, commented on them, wrote books
himself. They took him for a God, accepted his laws, and
declared him their president. The Christians, you know, worship a *man* to this day,—the distinguished personage who introduced their novel rites, and was crucified on that account. Well,
the end of it was that Proteus was arrested and thrown into
prison. This was the very thing to lend an air to his favourite
arts of clap-trap and wonder-working; he was now a made
man. The Christians took it all very seriously: he was no
sooner in prison, than they began trying every means to get
him out again,—but without success. Everything else that
could be done for him they most devoutly did. They thought
of nothing else. Orphans and ancient widows might be seen
hanging about the prison from break of day. Their officials
bribed the gaolers to let them sleep inside with him. Elegant
dinners were conveyed in; their sacred writings were read; and
our old friend Peregrine (as he was still called in those days)

became for them "the modern Socrates." In some of the Asiatic cities, too, the Christian communities put themselves to the expense of sending deputations, with offers of sympathy, assistance, and legal advice. The activity of these people, in dealing with any matter that affects their community, is something extraordinary; they spare no trouble, no expense. Peregrine, all this time, was making quite an income on the strength of his bondage; money came pouring in. You see, these misguided creatures start with the general conviction that they are immortal for all time, which explains the contempt of death and voluntary self-devotion which are so common among them; and then it was impressed on them by their original lawgiver that they are all brothers, from the moment that they are converted, and deny the gods of Greece, and worship the crucified sage, and live after his laws. All this they take quite on trust, with the result that they despise all worldly goods alike, regarding them merely as common property. Now an adroit, unscrupulous fellow, who has seen the world, has only to get among these simple souls, and his fortune is pretty soon made; he plays with them.

Austerity and asceticism in Lucian's time were considered high virtues, not only by the nascent sect of Christians but by the adherents of the fashionable philosophy of Stoicism, in which Marcus Aurelius set an example. Among the philosophers, the will to refrain from any of the common joys and pleasures of mankind became that most insupportable form of snobbery—intellectual snobbery. It took the form of condemning as frivolous every form of art that was enjoyed by the populace. Not only did the Stoics and Christians frown upon luxury; they, according to Lucian, believed "that virtue consists in being uncomfortable." The Stoics maintained their blessed

gravitas, or the appearance of it, like a father who declines
to be human in the presence of his children, lest he lose
the tyranny over them he believes he is, by age and experience, entitled to.

The Stoics condemned, without ever going to see
them, the lively arts of dance and pantomime, as being the
recreations of the ignorant mass of common people. Lucian,
who was the most intellectual man of his time, was democratic in mind and spirit; and, since nothing human was
alien to him, he found the highest esthetic expression in
the very art the Stoic philosophers most utterly condemned—pantomime. The mere fact that a pantomimic
performance is, like a concert by Kreisler, ephemeral and
that the skill of a pantomimist dies with the artist, was no
reason to Lucian for ranking it below the arts of literature,
sculpture, painting, and music; for, as he points out, pantomime embraces them all.

Pantomime, he says, requires "the highest standard
of culture in all its branches, and involves a knowledge
not of music only, but of rhythm and meter, the subtleties
of dialectic alone being rejected as serving no useful purpose. Rhetoric, too, so far as that art is concerned with the
exposition of human character and human passions, claims
a share of its attention. Nor can it dispense with the
painter's and sculptor's arts; in its close observance of the
harmonious proportions that these teach, it is the equal of
an Apelles or a Pheidias. But above all Mnemosyne and her
daughter, Polyhymnia, must be propitiated by an art that

would remember all things. Like Calchas in Homer, the pantomime must know all 'that is, that was, that shall be'; nothing must escape his ever ready memory. Faithfully to represent his subject, adequately to express his own conception, to make plain all that might be obscure;—these are the first essentials of the pantomime, to whom no higher compliment could be paid than Thucydides' tribute to Pericles, who, he says, 'could not only conceive a wise policy, but render it intelligible to his hearers'; the intelligibility, in the present case, depending on clearness of gesticulation."

One of Lucian's favorite themes in the dialogues is that men, too often, strive after the wrong things in life—fame and money. Yet so far is he from rehashing the platitude that money does not bring happiness and that fame does not bring contentment, his argument is that disappointment and disillusion come only when these aims are consciously pursued. The accidents of birth, circumstance, natural endowments and inheritance account for much in the system of life, he contends; and in every pursuit or profession there are disagreeable aspects. It is the rule of life. In the *Cock*, which is a humorous handling of the Pythagorean theory of the transmigration of souls, he has the cock tell us all the states of being that so far have been his. In none of these has the cock found complete satisfaction, least of all the rôle of king. For when Micyllus (Lucian) asks the cock to tell of the felicity he enjoyed as a ruler, this dialogue ensued:

Mi. You tell me, cock, that you have been a king yourself: now how did *you* find the life? I expect you had a pleasant time of it, living on the very fat of the land?

Cock. Do not remind me of that miserable existence. A pleasant time! So people thought, no doubt: I knew better; it was vexation upon vexation.

Mi. You surprise me. How should that be? It sounds unlikely.

Cock. The country over which I ruled was both extensive and fertile. Its population and the beauty of its cities alike entitled it to the highest consideration. It possessed navigable rivers and excellent harbours. My army was large, my pikemen numerous, my cavalry in a high state of efficiency; it was the same with my fleet; and my wealth was beyond calculation. No circumstance of kingly pomp was wanting; gold plate in abundance, everything on the most magnificent scale. I could not leave my palace without receiving the reverential greetings of the public, who looked on me as a God, and crowded together to see me pass; some enthusiasts would even betake themselves to the roofs of the houses, lest any detail of my equipage, clothes, crown or attendants should escape them. I could make allowance for the ignorance of my subjects, but this did not prevent me from pitying myself, when I reflected on the vexations and worries of my position. I was like those colossal statues, the work of Phidias, Myron or Praxiteles: they too look extremely well from outside: 'tis Poseidon with his trident, Zeus with his thunderbolt, all ivory and gold: but take a peep inside, and what have we? One tangle of bars, bolts, nails, planks, wedges, with pitch and mortar and everything that is unsightly; not to mention a possible colony of rats or mice. There you have royalty.

Early in his career Lucian wrote an essay called *The Dependent Scholar,* which is a scathing indictment of the system of patronage, whereby an educated and talented man, out of fear of poverty, took residence in the house of a rich man, provided intellectual entertainment for the rich man's guests, instructed his children and gave dignity to his household—all in expectation of rewards in gifts to sustain him in old age. Lucian depicts stage by stage the progress and degradation of the dependent scholar in such circumstances, from the time he dresses himself in his best clothes and arrives at the patron's house "in fear and trembling lest you should be the first, which would wear an awkward air, just as it savours of ostentation to arrive last," until all that the scholar has to give has been exhausted, his soul crushed, his liberty obliterated, his self-respect made a thing of the past, until the patron "begins to look about for a convenient dunghill whereon to deposit you, and for an able-bodied substitute to do your work." This essay, like all of Lucian's work, displays an honest, unsentimental and unromantic facing of realities, a thorough understanding of human nature and motives.

In his old age Lucian was given a post in Egypt by the Emperor Commodus; and, lest some of the readers of *The Dependent Scholar* should censure him for accepting such a post as being contrary to the views he had expressed in his essay, he thought it necessary to publish *An Apology for the Dependent Scholar*. This is one of the autobiographical essays. It is also one of the last, if not the last, of his writings. It is not improbable that he died in harness in Egypt. In this "Apology" he tells us in an introduction that, *in appearance*, he is like "the quack who offered a cough-mixture which was to cure instantaneously, and could hardly get the promise out for coughing."

But his governmental post, he tells us, differs considerably from that of a scholar who accepts a position, which gradually becomes menial, in the household of a patron. His salary, which he tells us is large, comes out of the public treasury and not out of the pocket of Commodus. He is an important functionary in the government of the province of Egypt. "I control," he tells us, "the cause-list, see that trials are properly conducted, keep a record of all proceedings and pleas, exercise censorship over forensic oratory, and edit the Emperor's rescripts with a view to their official and permanent preservation in the most lucid, accurate, and genuine form." He was also next in line for the governorship of the province and, since he did not become governor of Egypt, we may take it that he died in harness of that gout which afflicted him in his later years and of which he made the subject of an amusing dialogue, turning his satire upon himself.

According to pious legend, Lucian was torn to pieces by dogs in divine vengeance for his skepticism toward Christianity. For centuries among the Greeks this manner of death had been the conventional legend concerning all those against whom the gods might be conceived to have a grudge. Actæon, the hunter, having inadvertently come upon the naked Diana bathing in a pool, was changed into a stag and torn to pieces by his own hounds. An apocryphal anecdote relates that the dramatist, Eu-

ripides, was torn to death by hounds because of the
impiety of his dramas. On the other hand, the legend of
death as the result of being torn by dogs had also a sacred
side in the legends of Greece. The harvest songs, including
the Linus song in the Iliad, lamented the deaths of boys
of extraordinary beauty who were torn to death by dogs;
and Linus himself, the poet-musician, son of Apollo and
Terpsichore, was supposed to have met his death in this
manner.

Aside from Lucian's autobiographical writings we
have one contemporary impression of him. I may lay claim
for my pointing to this bit of biography as a scholastic discovery, for I can find no authority on Lucian who has observed that the Lucius mentioned in the life of Herodes
Atticus by Philostratus,[4] is the Lucian of the dialogues.
That the Lucius referred to by Philostratus is our Lucian
I think there can be no doubt: Lucianus was the Latin
form of Lucian's name and Lukios was the Greek form.
Philostratus wrote in Greek. Lucian was a friend of Herodes Atticus, the rich philanthropist and public-spirited
citizen of Athens, who lived during the reigns of Trajan,
Hadrian and the Antonines.

Philostratus relates that Herodes Atticus so mourned
the death of his wife (for whose death, by the way, he
stood trial for murder but was acquitted) that he altered

---

[4] Philostratus and Eunapius, *The Lives of the Sophists,* edited with
an English translation by Wilmer Cave Wright, Ph.D., Loeb Classical
Library.

the whole interior of his house, converting all the decorations from rich colors into somber black.

And they say (writes Philostratus) that Lucius, a wise man, tried to give him advice about this, and since he could not persuade him to alter it, he turned him into ridicule. And this incident must not be omitted from my narrative, since it is held worthy of mention by learned writers. For this Lucius ranked among men renowned for learning, and since he had been trained in philosophy by Musonius of Tyre, his repartees were apt to hit the mark, and he practised a wit well suited to the occasion. Now, as he was very intimate with Herodes, he was with him when he was most deeply afflicted by his grief, and used to give him good advice to the following effect: "Herodes, in every matter that which is enough is limited by the golden mean, and I have often heard Musonius argue on this theme, and have often discoursed on it myself; and, moreover, I used to hear you also, at Olympia, commending the golden mean to the Greeks, and at that time you would even exhort rivers to keep their course in midchannel between their banks. But what has now become of all this advice? For you have lost your self-control, and are acting in a way that we must needs deplore, since you risk your great reputation." He said more to the same effect. But since he could not convince him, he went away in anger. And he saw some slaves at a well that was in the house, washing radishes, and asked them for whose dinner they were intended. They replied that they were preparing them for Herodes. At this Lucius remarked: "Herodes insults Regilla by eating white radishes in a black house." This speech was reported indoors to Herodes, and when he heard it he removed the signs of mourning from his house, for fear he should become the laughing-stock of wise men.

Here is another admirable saying of this Lucius. The Emperor Marcus was greatly interested in Sextus the Bœotian philosopher, attending his classes and going to his very door.

Lucius had just arrived in Rome, and asked the Emperor, whom he met going out, where he was going and for what purpose. Marcus answered: "It is a good thing even for one who is growing old to acquire knowledge. I am going to Sextus the philosopher to learn what I do not yet know." At this Lucius raised his hand to heaven, and exclaimed: "O Zeus! The Emperor of the Romans is already growing old, but he hangs a tablet around his neck and goes to school, while my Emperor Alexander died at thirty-two!" What I have quoted is enough to show the kind of philosophy cultivated by Lucius, for these speeches suffice to reveal the man as a sip reveals the bouquet of wine.

With this contemporary judgment of him I leave Lucian, the most contemporary of all writers of antiquity. He would have been at home with Heine and Anatole France, with Bernard Shaw and H. L. Mencken, with modern scientists and modern iconoclasts, with Professor Lane Cooper and Justice Oliver Wendell Holmes, with all urbane and disabused minds, who maintain throughout their lives a spirit of inquiry and of healthy doubt of the fabulous. He was a wit, a satirist and a humorist, whose comedy met that requirement of Meredith that it should be nurtured in serious thought.

APULEIUS

APULEIUS

*

LUCIAN and Apuleius were contemporaries. Both were Roman subjects in alien, conquered countries which were ruled by corrupt and extortionate colonial governors who insured the *pax Romana* and heavy taxes with garrisons of Roman soldiers. Lucian was a Syrian. Apuleius was an African, "half Numidian, half Gætulian" according to his own account, born in Madaura, brought up in Carthage and educated there and in Rome and Athens.

Lucian disdained to write in Latin, probably because he despised the Romans. He chose to write in Greek and the Greek he wrote was not in the ornate, involved and decadent literary fashion of the period but the clear, limpid Greek of the classical age, albeit his vocabulary and idiom were common to the man in the street. Apuleius learned Latin with great effort and wrote his masterpiece in it, in a lush, exotic style abounding in slang and neologisms.

It is in point to observe that, while little was being

produced in Rome that was of literary consequence, these two barbarians were giving birth to works of the imagination which the ages have chosen to preserve and cherish as supreme in their kind.

It is also in point to observe that these two original geniuses are so far apart in aim and method as to illustrate the opposite poles of philosophy that were then imperceptibly contending for acceptance. Apuleius was steeped in metaphysical doctrine; Lucian was a rationalist, actively inimical to all mysticism. Apuleius believed in miracles and magic and even stood trial on a charge of having won his wife, a rich widow, by magical means; Lucian exposed the tricks of the magicians with scientific thoroughness. Apuleius was initiated into the Greek mysteries and also, apparently, into the Egyptian mysteries of Isis and Osiris at a cost so great as to reduce his large patrimony to almost nothing; Lucian attacked the cosmogony of the Greeks with satire and ridicule. It was an age of both credulity and skepticism, of faith and unbelief, of faith-healing practiced by clever artists in legerdemain: "seriously it was debated, *teste* St. Augustine, whether Christ or he or Apollonius wrought the greatest miracles" (Whibley); Lucian had no faith whatever in any man's ability to transcend the laws of nature.

Both Lucian and Apuleius were athirst for knowledge—Lucian in a scientific spirit, Apuleius in search of an inner peace. In the *Metamorphoses* of Apuleius there is an indication in the XIth chapter that he underwent at

one time a profound religious experience, and although
he does not betray the ritual of the mystery of Isis (for
this was forbidden the initiate) his hero, Lucius, in sleep,
offers up a prayer to Isis and is answered by her; there is
a description of a religious procession in honor of the
goddess and a description also of the steps in an initiation
(omitting the "charge of certain secret things unlawful
to be uttered" and "what was said and done" that were
"necessary" and "convenient" but not to be disclosed to
the uninitiated); and finally there is this statement as
to the grace and ecstasy of vision which Apuleius' religious
experience had vouchsafed to him:

"I approached near unto hell, even to the gates of Proser-
pine, and after that I was ravished throughout all the elements,
I returned to my proper place: about midnight I saw the sun
brightly shine, I saw likewise the gods celestial and the gods
infernal, before whom I presented myself and worshipped
them."

When he, Lucius (or Apuleius), was finally given the
ultimate rites of initiation (after the discipline of fasting,
continence, bathing and anointment) he offered up this
beautiful invocation to Isis:

O holy and blessed dame, the perpetual comfort of human
kind, who by Thy bounty and grace nourishest all the world,
and bearest a great affection to the adversities of the miserable
as a loving mother, Thou takest no rest night or day, neither
art Thou idle at any time in giving benefits and succouring all
men as well on land as sea; Thou art she that puttest away
all storms and dangers from men's life by stretching forth

Thy right hand, whereby likewise Thou dost unweave even the inextricable and tangled web of fate, and appeasest the great tempests of fortune, and keepest back the harmful course of the stars. The gods supernal do honour Thee; the gods infernal have Thee in reverence; Thou dost make all the earth to turn, Thou givest light to the sun, Thou governest the world, Thou treadest down the power of hell. By Thy mean the stars give answer, the seasons return, the gods rejoice, the elements serve: at Thy commandment the winds do blow, the clouds nourish the earth, the seeds prosper, and the fruits do grow. The birds of the air, the beasts of the hill, the serpents of the den, and the fishes of the sea do tremble at Thy majesty: but my spirit is not able to give Thee sufficient praise, my patrimony is unable to satisfy Thy sacrifices; my voice hath no power to utter that which I think of Thy majesty, no, not if I had a thousand mouths and so many tongues and were able to continue for ever. Howbeit as a good religious person, and according to my poor estate, I will do what I may: I will always keep Thy divine appearance in remembrance, and close the imagination of Thy most holy godhead within my breast.[1]

In that magnificent last chapter of *The Golden Ass* (as I, following the example set by St. Augustine, shall call *The Metamorphoses* hereafter) we are given details of the ceremonies in worship of the most puissant goddess of that time, *circa* 150 A.D., namely that of Isis. One hundred and fifty years after the reputed birth of Jesus, the Christ, and in the very cities where Christian congregations had already grown up under the instruction and management of Paul and his associates, Apuleius, although he was a mystic and a Neo-Platonist, seems never to have heard of this new

---

[1] *The Golden Ass*, tr. W. Adlington, revised by S. Gaselee. Loeb Library, Bk. XI, p. 583.

religious movement which had sprung out of Palestine.[2]

The worship of Isis, however, had largely superseded the old religions of both Greece and Rome. "In that welter of religions which accompanied the decline of national life in antiquity," writes Sir James George Frazer, in the one volume, abridged edition of *The Golden Bough*,[3] "her (Isis') worship was one of the most popular at Rome and throughout the empire. Some of the Roman emperors themselves were openly addicted to it. And however the religion of Isis may, like any other, have been often worn as a cloak by men and women of loose life, her rites appear on the whole to have been honourably distinguished by a dignity and composure, a solemnity and decorum, well fitted to soothe the troubled mind, to ease the burdened heart. They appealed therefore to gentle spirits,

[2] The two passages in *The Golden Ass* which have been taken by some scholars to express a contempt for the Christian religion do not warrant any such interpretation. In Book VII, chapter 13, of *The Golden Ass,* there is this passage: ". . . and all they of the town of every age and sex gathered together to see this new sight and strange, a virgin in great triumph sitting upon an ass." This, say some scholars, is a parody of the Savior's entry into Jerusalem. Inasmuch as the ass is Lucius himself who had been transformed into that shape and the maiden was subsequently married, the inference seems far-fetched. Nor is there any good support in the text that Apuleius intended to represent the pestilent woman in Book IX, chapter 14, as a Christian on the strength of the line that she was "one that affirmed that she had instead of our sure religion an only god by herself." Her god appears to have been Bacchus.

Meanwhile it is also to be observed that, according to historical tradition, seven popes had reigned in Rome before the birth of Apuleius; the canon of Scripture had been fixed by the time he was twenty-five; the Jews again had been dispersed or put to the sword, the temple to Jupiter had been erected by Hadrian in a rebuilt Jerusalem; and four pogroms against the Christians had officially taken place in Rome.

[3] The Macmillan Company, 1922, page 383.

and above all to women, whom the bloody and licentious rites of other Oriental goddesses only shocked and repelled. We need not wonder, then, that in a period of decadence, when traditional faiths were shaken, when systems clashed, when men's minds were disquieted, when the fabric of empire itself, once deemed eternal, began to show ominous rents and fissures, the serene figure of Isis with her spiritual calm, her gracious promise of immortality, should have appeared to many like a star in a stormy sky, and should have roused in their breasts a rapture of devotion not unlike that which was paid in the Middle Ages to the Virgin Mary. Indeed her stately ritual, with its shaven and tonsured priests, its matins and vespers, its tinkling music, its baptism and aspersions of holy water, its solemn processions, its jeweled images of the Mother of God, presented many points of similarity to the pomps and ceremonies of Catholicism. The resemblance need not be purely accidental. Ancient Egypt may have contributed its share to the gorgeous symbolism of the Catholic Church as well as to the pale abstractions of her theology. Certainly in art the figure of Isis suckling the infant Horus is so like that of the Madonna and child that it has sometimes received the adoration of ignorant Christians."

It is generally assumed in scholastic circles that Apuleius wrote *The Metamorphoses* in his youth. Charles Whibley, in his vigorous and refreshing *Studies in Frankness,* places the date of composition of that "brilliant medley of reality and romance, of wit and pathos, of fantasy and observation" as in Apuleius' twenty-fifth year. But it seems to me that the textual evidence would indicate that it was written in his middle-life, probably somewhere around his fortieth year. The novel is a parable of his own experience and of his own search for peace of soul. This peace was achieved only after he had been a slave to the desires of the flesh and had been, symbolically, changed into an ass thereby. It was not until years of bitter experience and search for truth had given him wisdom that he was able to regain his pristine shape, absolved of sin, shriven of his errors.

It is likely, I think, that Apuleius was initiated into the various mysteries in his youth, achieving Osiris perhaps in his twenty-fifth year; but it seems more than probable that *The Golden Ass* was written in his meditative middle years. In support of this I would cite the close of *The Golden Ass:*

Finally after a few days the great god Osiris appeared in my sleep, which is the more powerful god of the great gods, the highest of the greater, the greatest of the highest, and the ruler of the greatest, to me in the night, not disguised in any other form, but in his own essence and speaking to me with his own venerable voice, commanding me that I should now get me great glory by being an advocate in the court, and that I should not fear the slander and envy of ill persons, which bare me stomach and grudge by reason of my doctrine which I had gotten by much labour. Moreover he would not that I should serve his mysteries mixed with the rest of the number of his priests, but he chose me to enter the college of the Pastophores, nay he allotted me to be one of his decurion and quinquennial priests: wherefore I executed mine office in great joy with a shaven crown in that most ancient college which was set up in the time of Sylla, not covering or hiding the tonsure of my head, but shewing it openly to all persons.[4]

Therein Apuleius says Osiris bade him get great glory as an advocate. Apuleius achieved this glory but at twenty-five he could hardly have known that he would, since he still had some years of travel, study, investigation and inquiry ahead of him before he settled down, after having rejected the priesthood, into being a rhetorician, lawyer, popular lecturer and man of letters.

The Golden Ass is not a work of immaturity, even of the immaturity of an extremely precocious writer. The flawless story of Cupid and Psyche which is embedded in it, is proof that it is not. That is a story which has enchanted readers in all ages from Apuleius' time down to our own; it has provoked imitation, inspired poets and dramatists and novelists, challenged the ingenuity of interpreters, and caused translators to labor over it with love. (Walter Pater in *Marius the Epicurean* called *The Golden Ass* "the golden book" and included in his novel his own exquisite translation of the Cupid and Psyche story from Marius' favorite writer.)

It is true, as Whibley points out, that the story of Cupid and Psyche in *The Golden Ass* is out of proportion to the rest of the novel; but as we shall see later on, it is the keystone of the structure. The novel, in the main,

---

[4] *The Golden Ass*, tr. W. Adlington, revised by S. Gaselee. Loeb Library, Bk. XI, p. 595.

is made up of a series of disconnected episodes and bits
of erotica, held together only by the itinerary of Lucius
in search of the magical meal of roses which would restore
him to human shape after he had been transformed into an
ass. One character only emerges vital and distinct, Fotis,
the jolly and sensual serving-maid; but there is a whole
tapestry pageant of thieves, ingenious lovers, depraved old
men, deceptive wives, pagan priests, witches, tradesmen,
soldiers, magistrates, and sorcerers, woven against a
somber, twilit background. Murder, mutilation, flagella-
tion, nocturnal horror, bats and specters contribute to the
sustained macabre effect of the first three and a half and
the last five books. Bawdy anecdotes which Lucian would
have presented in a witty and amusing fashion are related
by Apuleius in a manner at once precious and gross, provoking neither a chuckle nor a smile.

Apuleius is interesting, indeed, but not funny, however much he tries to mingle comedy with pathos, romance,
mystery and thrills. The reason is that Apuleius is essen-
tially a moralist and, strangely enough for his time and
place, a moralist of a peculiarly Pauline character. His dis-
trust of women amounted almost to a monomania. His
married women are uniformly lascivious and full of wiles,
often resorting to magic to gain their carnal ends and
cruelly resourceful in their vengeance when their wills do
not prevail. Matrons murder their husbands to gain easy
access to their lovers and to their husbands' fortunes;
others bewitch young men and, failing this, take magical

potions which transform them into fowl that they may
fly to the men they desire; others make mock of their
husbands' stupidity and give them horns in the most indecent and abandoned manner.

By converting his hero, Lucius, into an ass for having
drunk, by mistake, one of the magical potions used by
an adulterous wife in her escapades, Apuleius hit upon an
excellent device for visiting the moral opprobrium upon
ordinary human conduct that he had gained as an ascetic
and tonsured priest of Isis. As an ass Lucius is witness
to a great deal of behavior of which he seriously disap-
proves. Often he wants to cry out, but all he can achieve
is the first word of the sentence he wants to utter; and
this word is taken as a bray: no attention is paid to it.
So Lucius in his avatar as an ass kicks the top of a hogs-
head off to disclose to a husband his wife's paramour and
shows his distaste for breaches of monogamy by all the
overt actions performable by a morally censorious donkey.

Apuleius, indeed, is, like Baudelaire, fascinated and
repelled by evil, and in his spirit we see working some of
that ferment which produced among early Christian adherents that mortification of the flesh and that apprehen-
sion of supernal forces, both malign and angelic, which
resulted in the Manichean doctrine of the invisible war
between Good and Evil, set St. Augustine in his middle
years to retaste and repudiate his past, and made St. Sim-
eon Stylites sit for years upon a pillar in mortification of his
flesh to show a gaping crowd below what an awful heller he

would be if he gave in to the devil that was tempting him.

Yet there was this in Apuleius—that he had a notion that love might be physical, pleasurable and innocent like the love of Lucius and Fotis, or spiritual, pleasurable and innocent like the love of Cupid and Psyche. He confused matters, I think, as Dante and many others after him confused them, by allowing that there was any necessarily conflicting difference between the two. There is only, it seems to me, a fusion of spirit and body, and when either part is in fault one and maybe two neuroses develop,— and rather splendid works of art such as *The Golden Ass*, the *Last Supper* and the *Mona Lisa* of Leonardo da Vinci, the sonnets and plays of Shakespeare, and, name, in contemplation of your own neurosis, whatever appeals to you as satisfying to your soul.

Apuleius' first name may have been Lucius or something else. Scholars have been unable to find out. He is sometimes called Lucius Apuleius because the hero of *The Golden Ass* is named Lucius and we know, from external as well as internal evidence, that *The Golden Ass* is, to some extent, autobiographical—but not to the extent that Apuleius was ever himself turned into an ass. Nevertheless, during his own lifetime he was regarded primarily as a thaumaturge and only secondarily as a lawyer, rhetorician, lecturer, philosopher and man of letters. Among the literate of the Middle Ages it was not doubted that he had undergone the physical transformation he ascribes to Lucius in *The Golden Ass*.

In the eighth book of *The Golden Ass* there is an account of the mendacity and obscenity of "an old naughty man, somewhat bald, with long and gray hair, one of the number of those lewdest dregs of the people which go from door to door throughout all the villages, bearing the image of the Syrian goddess, and playing with cymbals and bones, to get alms of good and charitable folk." This old rascal, whose male but perverted and effeminate associates in priestcraft he addresses as "my daughters," makes a prayer to "the omnipotent and omniparent Syrian goddess, to Saint Sabadius and to Bellona with the Idæan mother and to Venus with her Adonis." In petitioning *sanctus Sabadius* this foul fellow is addressing the Phrygian deity from whose name we get the Sabbat or the witches' assembly (it has nothing to do with the Kabalistic number seven or with the Jewish or Christian *sabbaths*). Sabadius or Sabazius (Σαβάζιος) was worshiped as the patron of licentiousness and even in our own time there are scholars who are profoundly of the conviction that in the early and Middle Ages, and even down to our own witch trials in Salem, there were witches and warlocks, worshipers of St. Sabadius, who had compacts with the devil.[5]

We know very little about the life of Apuleius beyond the rather meager information he gives us in the writings that have been preserved. We don't know his first name,

---

[5] Consult the *History of Witchcraft and Demonology* by Montague Summers in the "History of Civilization" series edited by C. K. Ogden,

when he was born or when he died. He tells us he was born in Madaura in Africa and the conjectured date is 125 A.D. He also tells us that his father was one of the duumvirs or chief officials of the city. North Africa was so prosperous in those days that a rebuilt Carthage rivaled Rome and Alexandria in luxury and splendor. It is permissible to infer that Apuleius' father followed the intelligent course of complying with the system of which he was a dutiful official and an ornament by extracting all the graft he could lay hands on; for not only was Apuleius educated at Carthage but he was heir to a large patrimony which enabled him to loaf leisurely through many years of making up his mind what he wanted to do in life. It is probable that the language he first learned to speak in his home was Punic and he tells us that he was taught Greek in Carthage. It was natural then that he should go to Athens to continue his education rather than to Rome.

In Athens the profession of sophistry or skill in argumentation was so rife that it ranked with soothsaying and divination as a means of fame and livelihood. In a debased and impoverished city, culture still counted as a social asset; the academies inaugurated by Plato and Aristotle still carried on under the æges and endowments of the founders even though the founders would no longer recognize the stuff that was being taught in their names. The academicians had to meet a lively competition in the vari-

New York: 1926. Mr. Summers, an ardent Roman Catholic, does not doubt the reality of witchcraft. See also *The Witch-Cult in Western Europe* by Margaret Alice Murray, Oxford, 1921.

ous priesthoods which were prepared to offer degrees of initiation at augmented prices. Apuleius, having learned Aristotelian rhetoric and neo-Platonism in the academies, was still athirst for knowledge and shot his wad (or most of it) learning the hocus-pocus of the priesthoods. There were more of these then in Greece than there now are of Protestant churches and he, being an inveterate joiner, got into every one of them. After having gone through more degrees than the Masons or Knights of Pythias have to offer, he was as greedy for more as a modern self-made man is for collegiate honors. So, after having got pretty high up in the mysteries of Isis at Corinth, he proceeded to Rome to be further initiated and returned to Greece to receive the knowledge (and long hair and tonsure) of a priest of Osiris. Thence he traveled to Samos and Hieropolis in Phrygia and to Alexandria in Egypt, still hungry for initiation.

He arrived near home at last at Oea, close to the present site of Tripoli, broken in health and pocketbook from so much pursuit of knowledge. He had also been generous with his money to his friends, and Pontianus, a schoolmate of his in Athens, who put him up and took care of him in his illness may or may not have been a recipient of Apuleius' generosity. However, Apuleius was no sooner on his feet than Pontianus suggested that Apuleius marry his (Pontianus') widowed mother. If this sounds queer that a young man should ask his schoolmate please to marry his mother who was much older than

either of them one should look into the then existing
Roman laws of property which we and the English have
taken over with little humane modification.

The suggestion promptly sent Apuleius into a decline,
whereat Pudens, a brother of Pontianus, who was also
eager to participate in the inheritance of his mother and,
through her, his grandfather, hurried to Oea and took
Apuleius into his home where Apuleius spent a year con-
valescing, earning his keep by tutoring the household.
When he was well, Apuleius sought to make capital of the
instruction in rhetoric, grammar, literature and sophistry
he had had in Athens (he seems to have given up the
idea of the priesthood, probably because of the number in
which he was initiate) and arranged to give a public lecture. This venture was a huge success and it started him
on the road of becoming probably the most successful
public speaker of his time—a regular William Jennings
Bryan of the Roman Chautauqua circuit, with a schedule
including Carthage, Rome, Corinth, Athens, Antioch,
Alexandria and intermediate points.

Apuleius' success as an orator fired the resolve of
Pontianus and Pudens that Apuleius should marry their
mother and this Apuleius agreed to do because he had
come to love Pudentilla,—so much so in fact that he had
allowed her sons to arrange the marriage contract whereby
Apuleius was to receive a moderate dowry (300,000 sesterces) "on condition that this should revert to Pontianus
and Pudens in case she bore Apuleius no children; in case

she did, it should be divided among the children of her two husbands." [6]

Apuleius' marriage plunged him into hot water. Pudens was turned against him by relatives who wanted a share in Pudentilla's fortune and Apuleius was brought to dock on the absurd double charge of having murdered Pudentilla's second husband and of having won Pudentilla's love by magic in order to seize her fortune. The murder charge was dropped but Apuleius stood trial on the other count. He pleaded in his own defense and fortunately we have his answer to his accusers in the *Apologia*.[7]

The *Apologia* shows that Apuleius was a brilliant and witty orator, clearing himself superbly with humor and showing up Pudentilla's relatives with deadly malice as venal legacy hunters who had trumped up the charge of witchcraft.

We do not know when Apuleius died, but it appears that he rounded out his days in Carthage as a successful lecturer, special pleader and man of letters. Examples of his versatility in the use of language are to be found in the *Florida*.[8] His fame was great throughout the Middle Ages and the Renaissance both as a writer and as a necromancer; he was considered the equal of Virgil in the latter by those who believed *The Golden Ass* to be an exact account of his experiences.

[6] Elizabeth Hazelton Haight, *Apuleius and His Influence*, "Our Debt to Greece and Rome" series; Longmans, Green & Co., New York, 1927.
[7] Translated by H. E. Butler, Oxford Press, 1909.
[8] Translated by H. E. Butler.

ARETINO

ARETINO

*

PIETRO ARETINO, called "the divine" and "the scourge of princes" by Ariosto, was in his day at once the most celebrated and the most notorious man of an illustrious and dissolute century. He was a friend of all the great, the powerful, the infamous and the talented of his time, among whom were Michael Angelo, Titian, Raphael, Alessandro de Medici, the Emperor Charles V, Philip, King of Spain, Francis I of France, and the Popes Julian III, Leo X, Clement VII and Paul III.

He was a poet, a pamphleteer, an art critic, a wit, a satirist, a blackmailer, a flatterer, a soldier and a Don Juan. For twenty-two years, supported by pensions and gifts from emperors, popes, kings, princes and cardinals, he enjoyed rent free from a wealthy patron a magnificent palace on the Grand Canal in Venice, wherein he housed in apparent amity some thirty or forty women who adored him. He conceived a passion for the wife of Giovanni Antonio Sirena, whose daughter he had held at the baptismal font, and when that exclusive lady declined, somewhat reluctantly, to be confounded with the other inmates of his prodigious harem, he wrote to her husband protesting against so unprecedented a slight upon his *amour propre:* "Learn you, sir, that popes, kings and emperors think themselves happy when I desire to keep on good terms with them. Do you know that the Duke of Ferrara has sent me an ambassador with money because I would not go to pay him a visit? Do you know that there is not a woman in the world who would not be proud to be chastely sung and celebrated in my verses?"

In this he was not boasting, he was speaking literally the truth. He had the ecclesiastical, military, social and artistic world at his feet. He would have been made a cardinal if a political issue had not decided otherwise; he sat for a portrait by his crony, Titian; he corresponded with Michael Angelo, who considered him, as he was, the greatest art critic of his time; he was the confidential spy of Charles V and Francis I (both enemies of his native Italy); he refused the Strozzi Palace in Florence offered him by Alessandro de Medici; he was so entertaining a guest that the Cardinal de Medici was jealous when he remained too long with his host, the Marquis of Mantua; he was the author of a series of dialogues, after the manner of the Mimes of Herodes (or Herondas), which are models of objective naturalism; he was the first great emperor of the Fourth Estate in Europe, and he wrote some sonnets of so obscene a nature that they have probably never been equaled by any poets except Martial and the Hindus.

He was, in fine, Casanova's peer in amour, Cellini's in blackguardism, and Machiavelli's in pragmatic individualism, and he possessed a kind of literary genius which was foreign to them all, save Cellini, who was articulate (except for his memoirs) in gold, silver and bronze, rather than in prose and verse.

Last, and not least, he was a man of religious sentiments, exemplary piety and paternal solicitude. The scourge of princes, feared by the powerful, he was a friend, protector and benefactor of the weak, the penniless, the outcast and the lowly. True enough, he was maintained in luxury by the rich and influential and robbed and imposed upon on every hand by the homeless rabble he fed, clothed and sheltered; but he never faltered in his charity. He gave to the poor as long as he could exact tribute from the rich, and he was host to beggars, waifs, students, prostitutes and cripples at the table where often enough he declined to meet dukes, cardinals and profiteers who paid for what he ate and where he ate it.

He retained a confessor whom he doubtless kept busy; he was a prodigal, considerate and understanding mate of his numerous women, and he was a thoughtful, adoring and provident father to his children. When the time came for the christening of his daughter, Adria (by Caterina Sandella, who had left her husband to become queen consort of his harem), he wrote to Father Sebastino:

Although, Father, there is no need of new ties to unite us two, who are already like brothers, yet I have wished to bind us still further with those of the office of godfather, that they may ornament with their benign and sacred customs the friendship which virtue itself has established eternally between us. It has pleased God that the child should be a girl, while I, in the usual manner of fathers, looked for a son—just as if a girl (always excepting there be a doubt in her virtue, which we must see to carefully, that it be of the best) were not the greater consolation to us. For it is like this: a boy at about his twelfth or thirteenth year begins to pull at the parental curb and, breaking loose from school and obedience, brings causes for heaviness to those who have begotten him and given him birth. And, what is more weighty still, there are the threats and abuse with which he assails his father and mother day and night, from which ensue the chastisements of the law and of God. But a girl is the soft couch which gives repose to the hoary years of those who have begotten her, and never an hour passes but brings pleasure to her parents because of her gentle ways and her diligent care and solicitude for their needs. So that when I had expelled the vexation that came to my heart on seeing that the child was not in my image I became so vanquished by the tenderness of nature that I experienced to the utmost the sweetness of fatherhood. And it was the fear that she might die before tasting many more days of life which led me to have her baptized in my home, with a gentleman to hold her as your proxy, in accordance with the Christian custom. But I contrived the affair rather hurriedly, because from hour to hour we believed she would fly away to Paradise. But Christ has preserved her to be the diversion of my later years and for a witness to the life which others gave to me and which I have passed on to her. For which I render Him thanks, praying that He may continue my life until the time that I shall celebrate her marriage. Till then I must submit to being her plaything; for what are we fathers but the buffoons of our children? They trample upon us in their innocence; they pull at our beards, beat with their fists in our faces, ruffle our hair, and in such coin sell us the kisses and embraces which bind us. But what could be comparable to these satisfactions if only the dread of some misfortune befalling them did not keep our minds uneasy from hour to hour? Every childish tear they shed, every cry they give vent to, every sigh which comes from their lips or breasts brings agitation to our hearts. . . . In such wise is the sweet strangely compounded with the bitter. And the prettier they are the more acute is the dread of losing them. God preserve to me my daughter, for she is the most engaging creature imaginable, and my life would fail me if she were to suffer, much more to die.

After so affectionate a tribute it is a pain to learn that Adria caused her adoring father no end of trouble and anxiety. Titian had said that in her budding womanhood no one had so attractive a face as Adria's; and her almost omnipotent parent had seen to it that she was married off properly to a rich man in Urbino. Aretino had made dukes and princes contribute to her dowry and had had medals struck in her honor. But Diovatelli Rota, who had espoused Adria, refused to leave the house until the whole sum of the promised dot was paid over, together with a gold chain Philip of Spain had given Aretino, and immediately he got Adria under his thumb he began so seriously to mistreat her that she was forced to seek protection from the Duchess of Umbrino.

Aretino was capable, too, of something approaching the grand passion. Midway in his polygamous career one of his secretaries, Polo Bartolini, married an exquisite creature, by name Pierina Riccia. Aretino's chief consort, Caterina, brought the young bride and groom to Aretino's villa, on the banks of the Brenta; but shortly afterward Polo deserted both his wife and his master. Pierina was fragile, and in her disappointment fell ill of consumption. Aretino attended her with tender affection, enduring long journey after long journey through the wind and snow and horrible roads of a terrible winter in order to be near her and nurse her back to health. With such marvelous care she got entirely well. He returned with her to Venice and loaded her with presents. But no sooner were they established in town than she sneaked out of his house to depart with a younger man. She returned four years later, mortally ill, and he took her in and nursed her as before; but in vain, for she died too soon to requite his passion.

"Caterina Sandella and Pierina Riccia," writes Edward Hutton in his biography, *Pietro Aretino,* "would seem to have been the two chief women in his life; but his lighter and more evanescent love affairs were innumerable." He had, unquestionably, a powerful attraction for women; but now and then they betrayed him, for he was a very busy man. One of the women of his ménage, Marietta d'Oro, seemed irked by her lot and, in order to persuade her to stay, Aretino promised her a husband and succeeded in marrying her to one of his secretaries, a twenty-year-old youth. Then he sent the husband on a dangerous mission and accompanied him part way to make sure that he would go. When Aretino returned he found that Marietta had looted his house and set sail for Cyprus.

"All Venice mocked him. Meanwhile the young husband, having obtained the money from Francis, on his way back had lost it all at play, in the presence of Cardinal Gaddi, to Rohan. Aretino did not despair; he forced the Cardinal to make good the loss."

This is, as you will have seen, tragi-comedy, on the grand scale, involving as chief personage one of the most energetic and interesting personalities in history. It is a pity that Mr. Hutton did not take greater advantage of his opportunity, for he has given us, I believe, the first biography of Aretino in English. What he relates is fascinating enough; it is felicitously put with just the proper note of irony; it is, all in all, a delicious recital so long as it adheres to the facts. The trouble is that it stops short of being either an adequate or a wholly truthful biography. It leaves too much to inference; it is sometimes confused in the sequence of incidents and it somewhat slurs over Aretino's contribution to literature, which is considerable.

Why he did this I do not know, for so long as he has seemed to translate almost word for word, without credit, numerous paragraphs from Guillaume Apollinaire's monograph on Aretino, I, for one, should have congratulated him if he had translated more copiously. Apollinaire's biography is shorter, but it gives us more pertinent facts. Mr. Hutton has achieved a lengthy *jeu d'esprit;* Apollinaire has been almost as entertaining, though probably not so discursive, and has, moreover, told us any number of things that Mr. Hutton hasn't. Last of all, Apollinaire is not under Mr. Hutton's frequent compulsion of apologizing for the man, who is manifestly of extraordinary interest as a spectacle, whatever his divergence from the contemporary code. Apollinaire accepts him.

Among the people and the petite bourgeoisie of France, says Apollinaire, Aretino has been, in effect, a great moral force: "son nom évoque, avec ceux de Boccace et de Béranger, la grivoiserie qui est toute le santé et la sauvegarde du mariage. C'est que la variété est bien la seule arme que l'on posséde contre la satiété. Et l'homme qui, directement ou indirectement, a fourni à l'amour un prétexte pour ne point lasser devrait être honoré par tous les amants et surtout par les gens mariés." For Aretino, in his dexterous verses and witty dialogues, has informed many a married couple of the things they ought to know.

Mr. Hutton accepts a bit too readily, I think, Alessandro Luzio's refutation of Aretino's boast that his mother was a harlot and his father a man of rank. True enough, Mr. Hutton makes the literary point that such was the temper of the times that a man like Aretino "vastly preferred to be thought the bastard of a gentleman than what he was, the legitimate production of a shoemaker." But since Luzio succeeds only in establishing that Aretino's mother, the courtesan Tita, was married to a shoemaker by the name of Luca, I see no reason why we should not accept Aretino's boast. Luca may have been Sgnarelle.

For his mother Aretino had, obviously, a genuine affection, and Mr. Hutton's interpretation of the episode of
the portrait of the Virgin Annunciate is to me the most
surprisingly illogical thing in his book. Mr. Hutton sides
with Aretino's enemies in assuming that this was an
atheist's blasphemous defiance of churchly sanctities,
whereas it is to me an earnest of a touching and pious
filial devotion.

In the cathedral of San Pietro, in Florence, Aretino
had seen an artist's idea of the likeness of the Virgin
Annunciate and he had been impressed by its remarkable
resemblance to his mother. He forthwith ordered a copy
made by the mediocre artist, Lappoli, and, not satisfied
with it, engaged Vasaria to make him a more faithful
reproduction. This portrait he kept near him throughout
his life, showing it to friends and acquaintances.

It was Francesco Doni, a traitorous friend, whom
Aretino had protected, who gave rise to the calumny attached to the episode. "You are an Anti-Christ, a limb of
the Great Devil," Doni wrote to Aretino. "One sees the
picture of the Virgin Annunciate that you have in your
rooms, the portrait painted by Messer Giorgio Vasari that
he was made by you to copy because you said it was
an effigy of your mother. So to all you say: 'This is my
mother,' showing the Madonna. Thus you compare yourself to Jesus Christ, just like Anti-Christ." But Doni was
a fool; one may be a scoundrel and still love his mother
and liken her in his eye to the Mother Immaculate. In-

deed, therein lies the force and beauty of the Madonna worship.

There are two other points in Mr. Hutton's introductory summary of Aretino's life which are at variance even with the facts as he himself presents them later on, i.e., that Aretino was "kicked out of Rome for writing the notorious Sonetti Lussuriosi" and that Aretino died "as a dog dies, without a thought of repentance in the midst of a howl of blasphemy and laughter."

Aretino's quitting Rome had nothing to do with his licentious sonnets; he had quarreled with the chancery officer, who had employed assassins to do away with him, and he was forced to flee for his life. If Mr. Hutton will unscramble his chronological eggs he will discover this truth for himself; for on different pages he has Aretino banished from Rome at the same moment to two different places, and for different reasons, one of which is erroneous. And Mr. Hutton himself has good authority for more correctly recording: "Pietro Aretino died of apoplexy on October 21, 1556. In a new document which came to light in 1875 we learn what we might have expected, that he died suddenly, and also that he was buried in the Church of San Luca in a new sepulcher near the sacristy, and that a little before dying he had confessed and received communion, 'weeping very much.' According to a popular tradition, he died of a great fit of laughter."

Indeed, it appears that Aretino rounded out his sixty-four years very happily. As late as 1553 he "left Venice,

passed once more by Perugia and was splendidly received
by the Pope 'with fraternal tenderness' and every one
seems to have tried to persuade him to take up his abode
in Rome." He went, however, to live with Leonardo
Dandolo in the parish of San Luca, on the Riva del Carbin.
He had pensions from Charles V and others amounting
to seven hundred and twenty scudi, and he was "ever receiving splendid gifts of money and goods which . . . give
him security." There is evidence in his letters, Mr. Hutton
solemnly tells us, that Aretino was often unhappy. But
who isn't?

Aretino acquired the soubriquet, "The Scourge of
Princes," by adapting to his own uses the freedom of
speech granted by the ancient festival of Pasquin on St.
Mark's Day, April 25. According to legend Pasquino was
an acrid and critical schoolmaster who had lived in Rome
during the fifteenth century and had been feared and
famous because of his tongue.

In Aretino's youth the name Pasquino had been
attached to an early Roman statue which had been ex-
cavated and set up in the Piazza Navona. "To this statue,"
writes Mr. Hutton, "it had become the custom to affix
learned squibs on the papal government and famous persons generally." But, until Aretino found better use for
it, the pasquinade had been merely the diversion of dull
scholastic pedants.

It was Aretino who made the pasquinade the instrument of free and anonymous criticism, satire, rebuke, ridi-

cule and libel—the forerunner of the modern scandal sheet and yellow newspaper. Pope Leo X had died and, as Aretino had attached himself to Cardinal Giulio de Medici, he put his pen and Pasquino to the service of his patron, libeling all the other candidates in the Conclave. "Aretino wrote pasquinades daily as the modern journalist writes articles, but with a fury and energy, perhaps a wit, certainly with a wealth of personal abuse unknown to the English press of our day; and by this means he became famous through the world." Aretino's candidate was not elected, but his pasquinades fulfilled the mission of all such efforts in our day as his; "it amused the cynical among the Signori and it roused at once the interests and the anger and expressed the worst instincts of the vulgar, the popolo. It also made him immense fame." When Adrian of Utrecht ascended the Papal throne after the death of Leo X he feared the pasquinade, chased Aretino out of Rome and suppressed the feast of Pasquin; but he died five months later and was succeeded by Cardinal de Medici as Pope Clement VII. From that time on Aretino's fame was secure.

Apollinaire, in his excellent introduction to the French translation of selections from Aretino's work, gives a concise history of the authentic, spurious and doubtful compositions. "Besides his admirable letters, his pamphlets and his occasional poems," writes Apollinaire, "he wrote a tragedy in verse, 'Orazia,' and five comedies in prose— 'Marsecalco,' 'Cortigiana,' 'Ipocrito,' the 'Talanta' and the

'Filosofo'—which have merits of the highest order. There is evidence to believe that the 'Ipocrito' was the proto-type of 'Tartuffe,' for Molière had come across that play in Grenoble. The religious works of the divine Aretino enjoyed a considerable vogue. . . . It has been said that Aretino was a great prose writer but a mediocre poet. I believe that opinion is not quite just, for Aretino was at all events a satiric poet of the first rank. Some of his pasquinades are not inferior to the finest passages in Victor Hugo's 'les Chatiments.' "

Mr. Hutton's tribute to the *Ragionamenti* is beauti-fully phrased and, I think, wholly justified. "Aretino's page is full of life, hard to read, spontaneous and yet packed tight, worked upon and forged, full of queer instances and odd comparisons, glittering with wit and every sort of comic exaggeration. Such work does not exist outside his pages. His successor was Rabelais, but also Molière. He has the robust joy of the one, but something of the intellectual charm of the other. He takes us not only in spite of ourselves but in spite of his own animalism and coarseness. . . . For all these dialogues, obscene as they are, are not lascivious, they have the vigor of life and are filled with action. 'I have spoken the truth,' it is Aretino's continual cry as it was Boccaccio's and now, as in their own day, no one can be found to believe them. It is per-haps unnatural to love the truth for its own sake. We think the truth, if it must be spoken, should be uttered with more seriousness, more modesty and with less inordinate joy; not in a shout of laughter, but with severity and sorrow. It is not perhaps our hypocrisy, but our nerves which insist upon this. We are less robust than they; we know as little of their huge laughter as of their enormous and violent gestures; we take our pleasures—and among them the rebuking of sin—sadly."

But Aretino's *Dialogues* are no more peculiar to the *cinquecento* than is Aretino, as you will discover if you will read Mr. Hutton's translation of snatches from these dialogues and then read Charles Whibley's translations of snatches from the *Mimes* of Herondas in *Studies in Frankness*. And Aretino is no more a monster of iniquity than has appeared in every age, including greater numbers in this one, wherein vast energy and considerable talent are occasionally put to fascinating uses not in accordance with the code. To those critics who express surprise at the gulf that seemed to separate Aretino's religious beliefs and his personal conduct, and see in this the peculiar corruption of that phase of the Renaissance, I would point out that the spectacle is no less prevalent in our own day. There are plenty of good people who profess Christianity without conscious hypocrisy and yet are far from ever practicing it. This is not to be wondered at: religion and ethics, like art and life, are separate matters.

FRIEDRICH NIETZSCHE

FRIEDRICH NIETZSCHE

✳

IT is one of those many paradoxical ironies to be observed in life that the most strident and relentless opponent of Christianity during the last century was also the most strident and relentless opponent of the mass movement which finally succeeded in officially abolishing Christianity within the borders of the huge state in which the movement functions.

Friedrich Nietzsche hated and fulminated against what he called the slave-morality of Christian teaching but he also hated and fulminated against everything that is represented by the Marxian doctrine. His "will to power" as he conceived it was for the superior man, the clever and ruthless warrior who was able to dominate, enslave, exploit and rule the mass; he thought the evolution of the "super-man" was being hindered because superior men were victims of the same "slave-morality" (*i.e.*, Christianity) that the "chandala" professed. He had the utmost contempt for both the proletariat and the bourgeoisie.

He did not live to see the Russian revolution, proletarian in character, triumph and set about the destruction of all religions. The very reasons he advanced why he thought religions—Buddhism as well as Judaism and Christianity—were inimical to the free development of the individual aristocrat were the reasons advanced by the communists why the workers of the world were enchained.

Much of Nietzsche could be used by the Soviets as texts for the promotion of atheism among the workers and peasants. The difference is that Nietzsche meant his doctrine for the education of individual rulers whereas the leaders of the Communists made immediate and practical use of it for the education of the masses. Lenin, Trotsky, Stalin and their associates happened to be the "super-men" of the new dispensation in Russia and their will to power consisted in a program to free the masses economically and not to enslave them as Nietzsche wished his aristocrats to do.

Nietzsche thought he was looking toward the future; in reality he was looking myopically into the past. He was a poetic and romantic visionary who neglected to observe that whereas history seemingly repeats itself it never repeats itself in precisely the same way. You may have a strong physical resemblance to your great-grandfather; you may display many of his traits of mind and character; some of the episodes in his career may be analogous to those in yours; but still you are not your great-grandfather and the circumstances of your daily living are vastly different from his.

Entertaining, as he did, the interesting theory that life is to be perceived esthetically, not morally, it is strange that he did not observe that life not only can be, but actually is, perceived by many *esthetically*, from a moral, an ethical, a religious, a scientific or even a mathematical point of view; and that while he was viewing life *esthetically*, his was a moral (or non-moral) and ethical (or non-ethical) point of view and he was, moreover, giving expression to ideas that were already in the air and that reached (at least in the two incidents I have recited) concrete realization.

Lenin was by any definition Nietzsche offered a superior man; he not only had a will to power but attained power; he was certainly not religious in the sense Nietzsche meant the word and he was as convinced as Nietzsche was that religions are superstitious concoctions and impostures; but the visions of perfection entertained by the two were diametrically opposed. One thought perfection could be reached through the individual only; the other thought that perfection could be reached through the economic emancipation of the whole mass of mankind. Lenin had much in common with the early Christians in aim and purpose: he and they sought salvation for the oppressed. It remains to be seen whether the fate of communism will be the fate of that early doctrine of the brotherhood of man which in triumphing became the means of denying the doctrine by murders, wars, persecutions and intolerance.

However, to read Nietzsche during male adolescence is, I should imagine, a valuable and happy experience; for Nietzsche with his poetic doctrine of the will to power gives the diffident youth a feeling of reassurance. I know of one lad to whom I recommended that he read some Nietzsche who was cured thereby of a sense of inferiority that had been so acute he was almost paralyzed for effort of any kind.

Nevertheless there is in Nietzsche a great deal of fustian and whistling in the dark. His attacks on Christianity, which were all the more violent perhaps because he was a descendant of several generations of Doctors of Divinity, have in them the validity of a Yea-sayer. A weak and ailing man much of his life, he celebrated the virtues of health and dynamic energy. The two great influences upon his thinking were Goethe and Schopenhauer, whose attitudes toward life were fundamentally different, Goethe being affirmative and Schopenhauer being dourly pessimistic. Another influence was Wagner, who at first seemed to Nietzsche to express in his music all the values which Nietzsche had tried to express in prose; but after Wagner wrote "Parsifal" Nietzsche thought the composer had betrayed his cause against the Christian morality. From these conflicting influences there developed that chaos in him which he said was necessary to give birth to a dancing star.

So much of Nietzsche is old hat now that it is curious to reflect how infamous he was once considered. During the war some one in the propaganda department of the British war office hit upon the idea that Nietzsche was responsible for the German slogan, *Deutschland über Alles,* and so cited Nietzsche in proof that the Germans were baby killers.

"On the strength of the fact that I had published a book on Nietzsche in 1906, six years after his death," wrote H. L. Mencken in the introduction to his translation on Nietzsche's *The Anti-Christ,* "I was called upon by agents of the Department of Justice, elaborately outfitted with badges, to meet the charge that I was an intimate associate and agent of the 'German monster, Nietzsky.'" The amusing irony of this is that the Department of Justice officers who harassed Mencken on the charge that he was an intimate associate and agent of the "German monster Nietzsky" had through sheer illiteracy given to Nietzsche the name which in fact he strove ardently to claim, because he disliked the Germans so much that he wanted to be thought a Pole. Nietzsche's sister tells us in her introduction to *The Birth of Tragedy* that he sought to trace his descent from a certain Polish nobleman Nietzsky who had obtained the favor of Augustus the Strong, king of Poland, and had received the rank of Earl from him. Frau Förster-Nietzsche intimates that her brother's efforts to establish himself as a Pole had little foundation to go on.

Nietzsche is a poet and a stimulant, however exasperating he may be to the pious or however contradictory may be his theses. He had courage and he exhorts the reader to take courage. He felt, as many feel, that much of the emphasis put by the Christian and particularly the Protestant churches upon prohibitions and denials were defeatist and crippling to life; that they killed the spirit and made people look rather toward the grave than toward activity; that in making a virtue of chastity they were striking at the very source of life; that in preaching pity they were demanding an unnatural response to the primal instinct toward self-preservation; that by implanting in the conscience of mankind a sense of sin they crippled the free and happy functioning of life, making people botched and afraid and perverted. And at least relatively all these things are true. But it is also relatively true that all of the fruits of civilized life—literature, music, painting, even thought itself—are contrary to or limitations upon the elementary instincts of nature as these instincts are observable, for instance, in the behavior of pigeons, canaries, deep-sea fish, jungle beasts, or even in domestic animals.

When Nietzsche in hyperbole or in poetic exuberance cries out "Live dangerously!" he probably had in mind for audience sedentary philologists like himself and not, surely not, gangsters, militarists, automobile racing drivers and others. And when he admonished men: "Women are only for the recreation of the warrior" and "When you go among women, do not neglect to take your whip," he was indulging in infantile braggadocio for which any wise and intelligent woman will have an indulgent smile.

Alzo Sprach Zarathustra ("Thus Spoke Zarathustra") is, even in translation, an extraordinary prose-poem, sonorous, elevating to the spirit, rich and challenging and strangely like the music of Johann Sebastian Bach. *The Birth of Tragedy* is a provocative but often erroneous essay on esthetics. Nietzsche chose largely to write in apothegms; and thus, as William Lyon Phelps once remarked about Emerson, in him the whole is less than the sum of its parts.

Another paradox in the life and thought of Nietzsche is that his healthiest, most bracing book, *Human All-Too-Human* (translated by Helen Zimmern in the English edition prepared under the direction of Dr. Oscar Levy), is the one that was written when he was in especially poor health. In this book he has orchestrated his aphorisms in arpeggios of grave and graceful beauty, running from profound observations to plays of wit and irony and into moods of deepest melancholy. In this book, written after his break with Wagner, the philosopher turns musician after lamenting that the musician (Wagner) had turned sentimental philosopher. We find in this book also that Nietzsche intended as well as expected his thoughts should reach only a few "choice spirits" whom he wished to make free men—that is, free from bourgeois checks and prejudices. . . . And that is precisely what the Marxists propose to do, not for a few "choice spirits" but for the generality.

Nietzsche had never noticed that the man who has nothing whatever has much more in common, psychologically, with the man in power than either has with the solid bourgeois. The man who has nothing is free in his speech and in his actions because, having nothing to lose, he does not have to conform to the social dictates of the middle class. The man who is sure of his power is in the same case: he, like the man who has nothing, doesn't even have to read and therefore is quite often illiterate; his spirit resembles that of the longshoremen in earthiness and freedom from suppression.

J. M. Kennedy in his introduction to the English translation of *Human All-Too-Human* calls attention to a technique Nietzsche suggested in the famous aphorism 451, for stemming the rise of socialism. Writing in 1909 Mr. Kennedy remarks that statesmen and politicians already were beginning to have difficulty in meeting the argument of Socialism and so he offers them No. 451:

JUSTICE AS THE DECOY-CRY OF PARTIES.—Well may noble (if not exactly very intelligent) representatives of the governing classes asseverate: "We will treat men equally and grant them equal rights"; so far a socialistic mode of thought which is based on *justice* is possible; but, as has been said, only within the ranks of the governing class, which in this case *practises* justice with sacrifices and abnegations. On the other hand, to *demand* equality of rights, as do the Socialists of the subject caste, is by no means the outcome of justice, but of covetousness. If you expose bloody pieces of flesh to a beast, and withdraw them again, until it finally begins to roar, do you think that roaring implies justice?

Since Nietzsche wrote and, indeed, since Mr. Kennedy wrote, this suggested technique in Russia at least has been appropriated—and by the new governing class which overthrew the nobles. There the Socialists are no longer of the subject caste. The philosophical premise of the cynical Machiavellian suggestion is simply invalidated along with many other corollaries to Nietzsche's doctrine of the divine rights of the noble individual.

D. H. LAWRENCE

D. H. LAWRENCE

*

D. H. LAWRENCE was the most weakly endowed intellectually of the writers of major importance during the first two and a half decades of the twentieth century. He had the aberrant and defiant notion that the functions ordinarily attributed to the brain were, in fact, performed by the solar plexus and, in *Fantasia of the Unconscious*, without any trace of humor whatever, he expounded this notion with the utmost academic gravity.

When we consider Lawrence's efforts at ratiocination, as these efforts are poignantly visible in *The Letters of D. H. Lawrence* (edited, with an introduction, by Aldous Huxley), we may easily be persuaded that, in Lawrence's case, this freak of nature had actually occurred at his birth and that from his semilunar ganglia there proceeded those cock-eyed pronunciamentos and screwy generalizations we ordinarily associate only with the more intellectually deficient mammalia, such as ambassadors who owe their posts to the fact that their predatory records are so odorous that an obligated administration finds it convenient to get them out of the country, financiers who have clerks and secretaries to remind them what to think for publication while they are concentrating on how to gyp somebody, and demagogues who are swept into office by flaming appeals to mob hysteria.

Lawrence, born the son of a miner on September 11, 1885, in Nottinghamshire and graduated with a scholarship which enabled him to become a pupil teacher in the village of his birth, was (or became) a snob. Never a snob of the sort which he had every right to be, a snob who is aware that he is an intuitive artist, prophet and delineator of some of the profoundest phases of human emotions, but the sort of snob who bowed the knee to whoever had, by hook or crook, got into the peerage, or had an ancestor sufficiently venal to allow his descendants the luxury of communion with the better endowed of the lower classes.

There is, in Lawrence's letters to women of title in England, a sort of fawning obsequiousness, a false, flattering note, distressingly unlike the tone of his letters to those he considered to be in the same social class as himself. He assures them, these titled women, on every hand that they and members of their class are of superior clay—which must have been nonplusing to them, seeking as they were some surcease from the awful aridity their positions condemned them to, with husbands wearing themselves out defending the realm (and the hegemony of bankers and profiteers in raping the wealth of India and in sustaining the opium trade): in Lawrence, the *naïf*, they found (or thought they found) a direct, articulate demand that life find some richer meaning, savagely close to nature, in communion, conjugation, and emotional aliveness.

"I don't believe in the democratic electorate," wrote this collier's son to Lady Ottoline Morrell. "The working man is not fit to elect the ultimate government of the country"; and to Lady Cynthia Asquith he wrote to assure her that people of her station ruled by divine right, "Let us have done with this foolish form of government, and this idea of democratic control. Let us submit to the knowledge that there are aristocrats and plebeians born, not made." He forgets the kingly caprice and convenience which elevates to knighthood a marauder, a privateer, a soap baron or scandal-monger and so perpetuates the happy aristocratic rule which contributes so remarkably to the unemployment problem in Great Britain.

Lawrence deplored the democracy of the Prince of Wales. On the occasion of the Prince's visit to India in 1922 he had a criticism to make of the Prince's conduct. The criticism is thus paraphrased in *The Savage Pilgrimage,* by Catherine Carswell: "He would have had the king of England's son splendidly apparelled and dazzlingly escorted in such a way as to strike both worship and terror into his Indian subjects. The frail, sensitive, simple-mannered, well-meaning, but too often weary-looking boy would have gained a thousand-fold, thought Lawrence, by the very frailty and simplicity of his bearing, if he had

been framed in a magnificence symbolic of England and
England's throne.[1] Here were millions of men and women
who could understand glory and submit to it joyfully,[2] but
only if the glory was conveyed to them by the eye and ear,
by the richness of material stuffs and sounds and odours. It
is a sophisticated, moreover a Western imagination that
can be moved to the perception of the greatest earthly
glory by the figure of a slender, clean-shaven youth with
a pale, gentle face, who wears the tailored jacket and the
creased trousers of Savile Row. The Prince's outfit for the
hottest day in Canada ought, in Lawrence's opinion, to be
fundamentally different from his public appearance in
Kandy. I would have backed Lawrence to stage-manage
the public appearance of his own Prince to the best advantage for any given populace."

From this comment by Mrs. Carswell we can see that
Lawrence, a collier's son, would have his prince be less
democratic than he is. And Mrs. Carswell, who was one
of the many women who mothered Lawrence, patted him,
figuratively, on the head for his presumption.

[1] And who was to pay for all this,—people like Lawrence's father
and the taxed and starving millions of India? England, at that moment,
was suffering from an acute depression. Strikes and starvation alone were
abundant. In practical matters men like Lawrence and women like Catherine Carswell give me the pip.

[2] Who says so,—the Indians or Lawrence and Mrs. Carswell? The
enthusiasm engendered by pomp has a very disagreeable way of turning
into bitterness and hate once the flags are furled, and the band stops playing, there is no food in the cupboard and there are foreign taxes to be met.
Gandhi in a loin-cloth on a morning after is more potent than the memory
of a bejeweled youth on an elephant. The Prince had sense to see this;
Lawrence didn't.

The caste system in England, indeed, functioned quite visibly to Lawrence's mental confusion. When he eloped with the Baroness von Richthofen (who was married and the mother of two daughters and a son) he wrote many letters to his confidant, Edward Garnett, emphasizing the fact that the woman he loved was a lady, an aristocrat, whereas he was a commoner. A sort of juvenile pride marks his information to Garnett that as soon as she can get a divorce he is to marry a woman of the German nobility.

Nor did Frieda von Richthofen or her mother, the baroness, permit him to forget that Frieda had loved "beneath her station":

"Oh, I must tell you how the Baroness von Richthofen 'schimpfed' me on Friday night. She suddenly whirled in here on her way from the Tyrol to Constance, stayed an hour, and spent that hour abusing me like a washerwoman—in German, of course. I sat and gasped. 'Who was I, did I think, that a Baroness should clean my boots and empty my slops: she, the daughter of a high-born and highly-cultured gentleman'—at the highly-cultured I wanted to say 'I don't think!' 'No decent man, no man with a common sense of decency, could expect to have a woman, the wife of a clever professor, living with him like a barmaid, and he not even able to keep her in shoes.' So she went on. Then in München, to Else, her eldest daughter, says I am a lovable and trustworthy person. You see, I saw her off gracefully from the station." [3]

[3] *The Letters of D. H. Lawrence,* p. 49.

That is the detached artist speaking in those last two sentences. In many things Lawrence was an imbecile but in art he was a loyal and tortured slave. The love he bore for Frieda von Richthofen was an intensely enduring and passionate one, alternating even in its first stages between the extremes of tenderness and violence, which was, to him, the passional requisite for keeping alert and alive. Ascetic really by temperament, "weaned" from his mother, according to his own admission, only after his twenty-second year, monogamous and faithful to his elected mate, he was at once sadistic and masochistic and was made happy, apparently, only when he and Frieda were lacerating each other with abuse.

For more than a century, from the time of the Reform Bill, the mass spirit in Great Britain, articulate and inarticulate, like the mass spirit of France and of the United States of America, had been centered upon the hope of freedom and equality, true democracy, and a fuller life for each and every one; but money, power from brigandage in England (and to a much lesser extent in America) led to the establishment of a rigid caste system wherein, in successive degrees, those in one class could snub and patronize those immediately "inferior" while deferring to those immediately "above." The full potency of these artificial distinctions are manifested in Lawrence's attitude: "as Frieda says, I am common, and as you say, one-fifth the Cockney. I find a servant maid more interesting as a rule than a Violet —— or a Grace ——. After all,

I was brought up among them.[4] But Frieda is a lady, and I hate her when she talks to common people."[5]

Put your palm over the bobbed-hair of Frieda Lawrence in the crayon portrait facing page 205 of the collected letters and you get an impression of a quite masculine person, more masculine by far than the profile portrait of Rupert Brooke. It is a Voltairean face, really, with pugnacity in the chin, firmness in the mouth, determination in the nose, humor in the expression and a calculating steeliness in the eyes. "There's a woman," you say instinctively, "it would be very hard getting the best of." Then look at a portrait of Lawrence, pale, frail, ascetic, the sort of man that brings violently to the surface those "mothering" instincts in women, particularly those who haven't experienced motherhood. "Why do women fall in love with me?" he cried, youngishly, sincerely, when his cousin, whom he had eyed, showed signs of doing so.

Throughout his life women fell in love with him or at least with what they thought he represented; for Lawrence was a strict monogamist and all the efforts of other women to win him away from Frieda Lawrence were fruitless.

[4] *The Letters of D. H. Lawrence,* p. 93.
[5] It is obvious, from this, that Lawrence doesn't even know why he finds a serving maid more interesting than a Violet —— or a Grace ——. He thinks it is because he was "brought up among them." It doesn't occur to him that they really *are* more interesting. Spiritually they are free beings quite uninhibited by the bourgeois afflictions of the middle-class and upper middle-class.

"To love," Lawrence wrote to T. D. D. in July, 1914, six days before he was married to Frieda von Richthofen, "you have to learn to understand the other, more than she understands herself, and to submit to her understanding of you. It is damnably difficult and painful, but it is the only thing which endures. You mustn't think that your desire or your fundamental need is to make a good career, or to fill your life with activity, or even to provide for your family materially. It isn't. Your most vital necessity in this life is that you shall love your wife completely and implicitly and in entire nakedness of body and spirit. Then you will have peace and inner security, no matter how many things go wrong. And this peace and security will leave you free to act and to produce your work, a real independent workman. . . . This that I tell you is my message as far as I have got any." [6]

This account of love as a deep and fundamental thing, a means of refreshing and revivifying the spirit, as an end to be pursued in itself but not played with or regarded lightly is expressed frequently in his novels, poems, plays and letters. Sex was to him the all-important thing but it was also, to him, a sacred thing and love to him was a religion.

"Once you have known what love *can* be," he wrote on Christmas Day, 1912,[7] "there's no disappointment and no despair. If the skies tumble down like a smashed saucer,

[6] *Letters*, p. 206.
[7] *Letters*, p. 89.

it couldn't break what's between Frieda and me. I think
folk have got sceptic about love—that's because nearly
everybody fails. But if they do fall, they needn't doubt
love. It's their own fault. I'll do my life work, sticking up
for the love between man and woman."

Yet, four days later he is writing to David Garnett,
"Do you think you might persuade one or two quite tender
young ladies to lionize me a bit when I get to England?
Frieda pulls all my tail-feathers out and I feel as if a little
gentle adoration would come remarkably soothing unto
me." [8] And elsewhere he complains that Frieda is jealous
of his writing—of anything that absorbs his attention
away from her.

But Frieda was free and dominant—the more masculine
of the two (if "masculinity" means anything except force
over force). "Mrs. D. H. Lawrence," writes William Gerhardi in *Memoirs of a Polyglot*, "when you first set eyes
on her, is the type of woman to gladden your heart. A real
German Hausfrau, you say to yourself, suits him down to
the ground, the intellectual, incompetent husband! The
reality, however, is the reverse of this. Mrs. Lawrence dis-
likes housework; her husband excels in it.[9] Lawrence, a
beam on his face, which was like a halo, brought dishes
out of the kitchen, with the pride of a first-class chef in

---

[8] *Letters,* p. 91.
[9] "He was able to absorb himself completely in what he was doing at
the moment: and he regarded no task as too humble for him to undertake, nor so trivial that it was not worth his while to do it well. He could
cook, he could sew, he could darn a stocking and milk a cow, he was an

his unrivaled creations: [10] no, as if cooking and serving your guests were a sacrament, a holy rite. . . . 'I don't say he hates you personally,' Lawrence contended (they were talking about Lord Beaverbrook, whom Gerhardi was defending—B.R.), 'but these men they are like vampires. When they see an immortal soul they hate it instinctively.' His eyes gleamed. 'With a terrible black hatred, and instinctively try to annihilate what is immortal in you.'

"At which remark Mrs. Lawrence trembled with rage and expressed her agreement with some violence, which seemed to me a waste of effort, since if she had met Lord Beaverbrook she would undoubtedly have bowed to the man's extraordinary charm. D. H. Lawrence, wincing at this display of superfluous emotion, said quietly, 'Not so much intensity, Frieda.'

"Mrs. Lawrence, perhaps living up to the elemental naturalness of her husband's heroines, replied: 'If I want to be intense I'll be intense, and you go to hell!'

efficient wood-cutter and a good hand at embroidery, fires always burned when he laid them, and a floor, after Lawrence had scrubbed it, was thoroughly clean."—Aldous Huxley in the introduction to *The Letters of D. H. Lawrence*. Let those males who are too prideful of their masculinity not set this down against Lawrence as evidence of femininity: he was a man with five senses acute—and maybe six—and satisfaction came to him from doing anything he set himself to do, with all his ability and all his concentration.

[10] This is what Lawrence meant when he talked so mystically about "coming through." His concept is often sensuous and sexual to a high degree and, in consequence many of his stories may be interpreted in Freudian terms that are, in the legal term, "obscene"; but a true "coming through" with him was often as much the satisfaction in scrubbing a floor clean or preparing an edible fish as finding completion in sexual desire.

" 'I'm ashamed of you, Frieda,' he said. Whereupon Frieda's hatred for Lord Beaverbrook transformed itself into hatred for her husband, and was soon a spent cartridge."

Lawrence's first great book and, I think, his greatest, *Sons and Lovers,* is more definitely autobiographical than any of the others, although all of his writings are an autobiography of his spirit. His was an arduous as well as an ardent pilgrimage in search of truth and peace. "One sheds one's sickness in books—repeats and presents one's emotions, to be master of them," he wrote A. D. McLeod in 1913,[11] and in *Sons and Lovers* he shed the sickness of his attachment to his mother. "I had a devil of a time getting weaned from my mother at the age of twenty-two," he wrote Edward Garnett also in 1913. "She suffered, and I suffered, and it seemed all for nothing, just waste cruelty. It's funny. I suppose it is the final breaking away to independence."

The theme of this book he has described with a lucidity and definitiveness unusual in novelists who undertake to tell what their books "mean": "It follows this idea: a woman of character and refinement goes into the lower class, and has no satisfaction in her own life. She has had a passion for her husband, so the children are born of passion, and have heaps of vitality. But as her sons grow up she selects them as lovers—first the eldest, then the second. These sons are *urged* into life by their re-

[11] *Letters,* p. 151.

ciprocal love of their mother—urged on and on. But when they come to manhood, they can't love, because their mother is the strongest power in their lives, and holds them. It's rather like Goethe and his mother and Frau von Stein and Christiana—as soon as the young men come into contact with women, there's a split. William gives his sex to a fribble, and his mother holds his soul. But the split kills him, because he doesn't know where he is. The next son gets a woman who fights for his soul— fights his mother. The son loves the mother—all the sons hate and are jealous of the father. The battle goes on between the mother and the girl, with the son as object. The mother gradually proves stronger, because of the tie of blood. The son decides to leave his soul in his mother's hands, and, like his elder brother, go for passion. He gets passion. Then the split begins to tell again. But, almost unconsciously, the mother realizes what is the matter, and begins to die. The son casts off his mistress, attends to his mother dying. He is left in the end naked of everything, with the drift towards death." [12]

Women in Love, The Plumed Serpent, Aaron's Rod and most of Lawrence's short stories seem to have flowed directly out of his subconscious. And his was a subconscious teeming with the impressions and experiences of an extreme sensibility. These novels are less about people than about intimations. He was, for all his years of sickness, a very vital man. The extent of his creative work

[12] *Letters,* p. 78.

during the comparatively short space of his life is sufficient to disprove the charge of vital deficiency so often
made against him.

The strongest support of this charge is in his last
novel, *Lady Chatterley's Lover*. In that novel, more than
in any other he ever wrote, there is a thesis—a preach-
ment, indeed—which brought into concrete terms what he
had been trying to express hitherto.

Basically Lawrence was a man who, having risen out
of a servile class, was astonished to learn that love can
be a pleasure. Generations had informed him, probably
even when he was yet in embryo, that there was something sinful in the urges of desire. He discovered pleasure
in passion and it was a revelation to him. He made a religion of it. He became a high-priest in the worship of
Astarte. He was Parsifal on the Venusberg giving the
voluptuous nymphs and nereids a quite unnecessary ser-
mon on the delights of the flesh. In *Lady Chatterley's
Lover* he was direct in his teaching. In that novel a woman,
who has been carefully reared in the genteel tradition, is
married to an asexual husband. She is physically attracted
by the game-keeper on her estate and deliberately sets
about to seduce him. He has been hurt by life and has
withdrawn into himself, "solitary and intent, like an ani-
mal that works alone, but also brooding, like a soul that
recoils away, away from all human contact. . . . He dreaded
with a repulsion almost of death, any further close human
contact. He wished above all things she would go away,

and leave him to his own privacy. He dreaded her will, her female will, and her modern female insistency. And above all he dreaded her cool, upper-class impudence of having her own way. For after all he was only a hired man. He hated her presence there."

This love-hate, hate-love concept about which Lawrence is ever insistent, is both simplified and intensified in *Lady Chatterley's Lover*. It seems to have been a concept in his mind which arose because of his consciousness of economic inferiority; for the game-keeper's first fear and hate toward Lady Chatterley arose because he felt that her will to get what she wanted was the result of her social and economic security. But, whereas Lady Chatterley at first experienced both a contempt and an attraction toward the game-keeper, she had an aversion from her husband which was not associated with attraction. "She felt she had always really disliked him. Not hate: there was no passion in it. But a profound physical dislike. Almost it seemed to her, she had married him because she disliked him, in a secret, physical sort of way. But of course, she had married him really because in a mental way he attracted and excited her. He had seemed, in some way, her master, beyond her.

"Now the mental excitement had worn itself out and collapsed, and she was aware only of the physical aversion. It rose up in her from her depths: and she realized how it had been eating her life away.

"She felt weak and forlorn. She wished some help

would come from outside. But in the whole world there was no help. Society was terrible because it was insane. Civilized society is insane. Money and so-called love are its two greatest manias; money a long way first. The individual asserts himself in his disconnected insanity in these two modes: money and love."

When Lady Chatterley sets about deliberately to seduce the game-keeper, her attitude toward him is that of a mistress toward a servant: she meant to use him only as an instrument subject to her will. But he, not she, is master of the situation; for with him she experiences for the first time in her life what physical love may mean.

But, "Once in her room, however, she felt vague and confused. She did not know what to think. What sort of man was he, really? Did he really like her? Not much, she felt. Yet he was kind. . . . But perhaps he wasn't quite individual enough; he might be the same with any woman as he had been with her. It really wasn't personal. She was only really a female to him.

"But perhaps that was better. And after all, he was kind to the female in her, which no man had ever been. Men were very kind to the *person* she was, but rather cruel to the female, despising her or ignoring her altogether."

Here, in the revery of Lady Chatterley, Lawrence is giving utterance to the profoundest resentment that women have against the order of things in this world. Highly individualistic women—that is, women very prideful of their ego—resent being regarded as mere instruments in what they call a "man-made" world, wherein things are so disposed that men can too easily remind them of their biological handicap.

There is irony in the fact that Lady Chatterley at first contemplated Mellors, the game-keeper, in much the same fashion that a female mantis contemplates (or is said to contemplate) a likely male of her species; but that when she thought she would use him merely as an instrument, something higher than herself—the urge of nature, the *élan vital,* the whatever it is that we know so little about and yet give to it high-sounding terms—she realized that it was not necessary that either men or women should regard one another as inimical.

Mellors is elemental and unsentimental; he is the "coarse" and factual; and yet in a true union he discovers to himself and to Lady Chatterley that there is, or may be, a deep and abiding happiness.

There is, of course, at least a temporary one in the solution Lawrence offers; but the end of his story is as much subject to dissension as the happy-ending of any Pollyanna story. Lady Chatterley is with child and she seeks a divorce from Lord Clifford that she may go to "some small farm of their own, into which he (Mellors) could put his energy." She tells her husband what has happened and asks for a divorce. He responds to this demand with the customary platitudes of a man in his situation and of his station in life:

"That scum! That bumptious lout! That miserable cad! And carrying on with him all the time, while you were here and he was one of my servants! My God, my God, is there any end to the beastly lowness of women! . . . You mean to say you want to have a child by a cad like that?"

"Yes. I'm going to."

"You're going to! You mean you're sure! How long have you been sure?"

"Since June."

The rest of the passage is high drama and the dialogue is imagined artistically. The emphasis, however, is not on the tragedy of the situation, especially as it affects Sir Clifford (who, after all, was not precisely responsible for his deficiencies) but on the thesis Lawrence wished to present: the thesis that men and women should make a religion of sexual satisfaction. He was very honest and sincere about this,—so honest and sincere, in fact, that what was at first a simple and cogent conviction became a mystical obsession. He could not bear to hear of sex treated lightly or in jest. Entirely without a sense of humor, he was, curiously enough (when we remember that *The Rainbow* was burned in London by the public hangman and *Lady Chatterley's Lover* has never yet been admitted to public sale in England or the United States), puritanical. He was outraged by any facetious treatment of the love between men and women. There grew up in his mind a bugaboo about what he called the "dark gods."

These gods, he said, should never be offended; and yet he fought with a Nietzschean intensity the Christian ideal of selfhood and the Christian ideal of morality. He wrote so enigmatically about "the dark gods" that Aldous Huxley, in his introduction to the posthumous volume of Lawrence's letters, was led into a similar vagueness of expression. Quite candidly I admit I don't know what Huxley is talking about in his mellifluous words about "Oneness and divine Otherness" or when he says "for someone with a gift for sensing the mystery of otherness true love must necessarily be, in Lawrence's vocabulary, *nocturnal*. So must true knowledge. Nocturnal and tactual —a touching in the night." I hope Mr. Huxley's meaning is perfectly clear to him; it isn't to me. Whereas I know of no person to whom the "message" of Lawrence's novels is not perfectly clear. That message is too obvious to require stating.

But it is not with the "message" that any one should approach as fine an intuitive artist as Lawrence, but with a mind willing to find or not to find pleasure in the world he created in his novels which was a world that is not to be found in the quaint records about him: *Lorenzo in Taos*, by Mabel Dodge Luhan; *The Savage Pilgrimage*, by Catherine Carswell; *Lawrence and Brett*, by the Hon. Dorothy Brett; and *Reminiscences of D. H. Lawrence* by John Middleton Murry—interesting as each of these books is in itself (and all for different reasons).

THEODORE DREISER

THEODORE DREISER

*

IN the Gospel according to Sigmund Freud it is re-corded as axiomatic that every great or notable achievement of the human spirit arises from an early ac-quired sense of inferiority and from heroic efforts to over-come it. When, through some physical or environmental handicap, real or imagined, a proud and sensitive child is made to suffer chagrin and embarrassment, his self-love, his ego, his vanity—call it what you will—comes to his defense, as an anodyne to his hurt, and directs his energies toward the accomplishment of some high aim which shall make his tormentors regret their actions and bend the knee humbly in admiration and respect.

Perhaps the most magnificent instance of a triumph achieved through the working of the sense of inferiority is to be found in the Old Testament, wherein we observe how a slave nation spiritually emancipated itself by con-ceiving its people to be the chosen wards of an Almighty Ruler, against whose protective and vengeful omnipotence

the most arrogant of temporal kings was nothing, and how
the very audacity of this dazzling concept captivated the
imagination of other races and made that concept grow
and prevail throughout the Western world.

The biographies of men who rise above their fellows
almost invariably reveal that in their childhood they bore
the pain of a quickening sense of the necessity to husband
great ambitions to compensate for the snubs, slights and
bullyings to which they must submit. The undersized Na-
poleon towered over Europe; Roosevelt, the school
weakling, bronzed himself on the Western plains, became
a mighty hunter, practiced his lungs for the bellow of the
Bull Moose, and gained his following as a man of tremendous strength and vigorous action. The psychology of
the Horatio Alger Jr. stories (and of the Elsie books no
less) is substantially sound: the rapid rise to affluence in
the one is initiated by the pinch of poverty and by the
scufflings which are the lot of the under dog, and the serene
self-satisfaction in the other is a consciousness of a spiritual superiority over those who are selfish, brutal, deceptive and coarse. It is important to observe, however,
that the sense of inferiority must be felt by a superior
person if it is to actuate great deeds: not all poor boys
become rich, not all weaklings become great men of action,
not all unhappy children become artists.

In fine, Freud's theory does not take into account
the special spark one must receive at birth in order to
attain a place above the general run of humanity; nor is

there any way of telling what direction that vital energy (which is to be differentiated from physical energy) may take; or to gauge the effect of chance. In America at the time of Theodore Dreiser's birth there were thousands of children being born under the same handicaps of poverty and physical disability that were Dreiser's lot from the fates. Few of these have ever reached any sort of distinction at all. Many have perished utterly. Dreiser alone has achieved the special sort of distinction of recording in novels, plays, short stories, essays and autobiographical writings a microcosm of life in industrial America which entitles him to be considered among the great writers of his time.

DAWN, which is the autobiography of Theodore Dreiser's early youth, is comparable in many ways to Rousseau's *Confessions*. In their youth Rousseau and Dreiser were temperamentally alike. Both were sensual and passionate, yet frustrated, awkward and diffident.

Both of them were plagued by desire and yet were burdened with an overwhelming sense of failure because of their scruples and their fright in the presence of girls and women. For a long time they both remained virginal and prurient; and they experienced the ecstasies of an ideal, unattainable love together with release in crude and obtuse carnalities. They were both brought up in poverty, dependent and living on charity, and they yearned for luxuries and an opportunity to shine in the world. They both had a horror of injustice and an excruciating sense of the inequalities existing in organized society.

Rousseau imagined that he was unique—"I am not made like any one else I have been acquainted with, perhaps like no one in existence"—whereas he was merely the first one like himself completely articulate about, and profoundly concerned with, the nature of his own soul.

Dreiser, as a child, was uncomfortably fearful that he alone was "sinful" or "depraved" and his early life was a long and painful experience in teaching him that he was not; his book is a protracted outcry against the bugaboos that haunted his conscience and kept him perturbed, ineffectual, and miserably lacking in courage and self-assurance.

Rousseau, when he started to lay bare his heart, wrote: "Whenever the last trumpet shall sound, I will present myself before the Sovereign Judge with this book in my hand and say aloud, Thus have I acted; these were my thoughts; such was I."

Dreiser says: "I will not say that this is a true record. It must substantiate itself. It is—as they say in law—to the best of my knowledge and belief. I may add, though, that these very sincere impressions and transcriptions are as nearly accurate as memory can guarantee."

After reading Rousseau's *Confessions* and Dreiser's *Dawn* it is impossible not to believe in the honesty and sincerity of their records. They have neither belittled nor exalted themselves: Rousseau's frankness is touching; Dreiser's humility is profound.

Both of them were brought up in an atmosphere of religious piety, and both of them by writing their confessions have attempted to exorcise, consciously or unconsciously, a deep sense of guilt, hanging over from their childhood and adolescence. Indeed, it would appear that we owe the *Confessions* of Rousseau largely to the furies of conscience he bore for so many years because of the beastly trick he played upon the young servant, Marion, whom he accused of stealing a piece of ribbon which he himself had stolen and thus brought about her disgrace and dismissal. We owe *Dawn* to Dreiser's sense of the wonder, mystery, beauty, terror and tragedy of life; but also, perhaps, to his having once been caught embezzling $25 of the funds he collected for an installment house.

Rousseau had his Monsieur de Pontverre, the vicar ("a bigot, who knew no virtue except worshiping images and telling his beads; in a word, a kind of missionary, who thought the height of merit consisted in writing libels against the ministers of Geneva"); and Dreiser had his dogmatic little Bavarian priest who was unfeelingly officious and callous at the death of Dreiser's mother. And these unfortunate brushes with poor representatives of the Catholic Church soured both men unreasonably against the church itself—indeed, helping to make Dreiser (who blames his father's religious mania and idle resignation for most of the family troubles) a fanatical anti-religionist.

Acutely sensitive to personal slights, indignities, and the handicaps of their poverty and dependence, both men developed adamantine characters which were highly individual, and which carried them relentlessly, stubbornly, uncompromisingly to their high destiny. For good or ill they are pathmakers in literature and they have contributed classics to the language.

Dreiser was one of thirteen children, three of whom died before he was born, in Terre Haute, Indiana, on August 27, 1871. His father was a German Catholic, born in Mayen, fifteen miles from Coblenz, and his mother was the daughter of a prosperous farmer of the Dunkard or Mennonite faith. Dreiser's father, a weaver by trade, had met the farmer's daughter while working his way from New York to Dayton, Ohio, and after a brief courtship they were married.

Dreiser's tribute to his mother for her tolerance, courage, spirit and love of her children is an eloquent and affecting one, recurring throughout the book. In poverty and disgrace, in sorrow and misery, she somehow kept her family together by superhuman labor, and all of the children, especially the boys, were dependent upon her spiritually and materially. They leaned upon her; she was in a way their hold upon life; they all felt disintegrated and dispersed when she died. Theodore was inconsolable and he faced life without her in greater terror and bewilderment than ever.

In writing his autobiographies Dreiser, it would seem,

is driven by a compulsion outside himself. He felt compelled to set everything down frankly and humbly. He says: "I can feel sorry for him who is so fearful of life and so poorly grounded in an understanding of things that he is terrorized lest some one discover that his uncle was a horse thief or his sister a prostitute or his father a bank wrecker, but I cannot sympathize with his point of view. What has that to do with me? an individual has the right to ask himself. And if he has sufficient consciousness of individuality, it has nothing to do with him. If he is over-influenced by conditions in which he finds himself, at birth or later, then, of course, they have a great deal to do with him, though it does not follow that they are a cause for shame."

In *Dawn* he spared his sisters public embarrassment by giving them fictitious names and rearranging their chronology, but in portraying them and his brothers he was as analytical and truthful as with himself. One of the few things in all of Dreiser's work that I had found unconvincing was the seduction of Jennie Gerhardt. Hereafter I shall be less skeptical; for it appears that one of Dreiser's sisters was seduced in precisely that manner. Dreiser's sisters have unburdened their souls to him.

Dawn carries Dreiser through his childhood and early youth. It is a record of his associations with people, the trials of his family, the beginnings of his thirst for knowledge and beauty and understanding, his reading and his studies, his odd jobs and his sentimental and sexual yearnings. It is a great book, a memorable and valuable one, destined I believe to become a classic of self-revelation. It has its pages of extremely bad writing; Dreiser's style is often as uncouth as Balzac's and as powerful.

Dreiser reaches no conclusions, except confused and contradictory ones. He recalls for what they are worth certain premonitions others claimed to have had; and he seems to be haunted vaguely by some intimations of a supernatural force, even when he can designate it no more fully than by capitalizing the "N" in Nature. He writes: "Nature, either necessarily or because spiritually it desires it (and I think the former is the case), is seeking an equation between extremes which would otherwise clash in enormous contests for dominance, the one to the exclusion of the other through æons of time."

The workings of this equation, indeed, are observable in Dreiser's own character and career. A determinedly realistic recorder of the behavior of life as he has known and observed it, he is at the same time profoundly saddened by the unjust war the strong wage against the weak and hopeful that, through some system of checks and balances in a socialized economic world, the power of the strong to wreak misery on the rest will be destroyed. In his youth he meant to seek a purely materialistic fortune in a country where the possession of money was the criterion of success, and instead he dedicated himself to literature from which, until he was long past middle-life, he derived only poverty and violent opposition from the entrenched panders of American criticism, all of whom were committed to the policy of denying the truth about the life that was making fawning slaves of them. He, himself a man of relentless energy and indominable will, nonmoral and individualistic, has been the most courageous crusader against the social misuse of energy and will.

After attending the parochial schools in Terre Haute and the public schools of Warsaw, Dreiser was persuaded by one of his school-teachers, an unattractive spinster whose memory he honors, to accept money from her for his tuition at the University of Indiana. This he did, but he found university life distasteful and unprofitable to him and he gave it up after one year. As a shy and moody boy in Warsaw he had taken refuge from reality in Dickens, Scott, Thackeray, Hawthorne, Fielding, Defoe, Cooper, Irving, Lew Wallace, Shakespeare, Dryden, Pope, Herrick, in that catholic disorder that is so repugnant to the disciplinarians of the schools.

On leaving the university he went to Chicago, where he worked at various kinds of menial jobs and, in experience, came to know the substratum of industrial and commercial life. He got into newspaper work somewhat by accident and, fortunately without ever distinguishing himself, he saw the life a reporter sees on various middlewestern dailies before he made up his mind to try his luck in New York. The story of the years—of his rebuffs, his expanding mind, his conversion to the materialistic philosophy of Huxley, Spencer and Tyndall, his determination to write novels after having absorbed nearly all of Balzac in a Pittsburgh public library, of his experiences with women, of the characters he met, of the writing of *Sister Carrie* and its fate, which caused him to abandon novel writing for ten years, of his hack-work and work as an editor of *The Delineator* he has told at almost excruciating length (because of the extraordinary vividness of his memory and his determination to tell the truth) in *Dawn, A Book About Myself,* and also in *A Traveler at Forty, A Hoosier Holiday,* and *Twelve Men.*

No one, indeed, has ever set out to record his life as relentlessly and as fully as Dreiser has. Criticism, so often hurled at him that he is verbose, no more deters him in his aim to be honest about the life he has known than does the criticism that he is a bad writer prevent him from building up his powerful novels of American life, such as *Sister Carrie, Jennie Gerhardt, The Financier, The Titan, The "Genius,"* and *An American Tragedy,* all of them teeming with authentic life.

Dreiser was the first American novelist to show men, boys, girls and women in the process of earning a living under industrialism, and, although many novelists and short story writers since him have depicted this process in certain fields, Dreiser alone has given us novels showing not only men and women at work but showing also the interrelation of these various activities. In fact, it was Dreiser's very attempt to give the *whole* of the lives of his characters that early in his career shocked what Emily

Dickinson called the "Dimity convictions" of puritan America.

Before Dreiser's time, novelists in the main wrote for, and about, people who lived upon income and who, because of this, were able to busy themselves in smoothing out the surfaces of life while ignoring what was going on beneath. Literature was a branch of "culture" and culture was a state attainable only by the "right people," *i.e.*, those who could subscribe to the opera and the symphony concerts and donate old masterpieces of painting to the municipal art galleries. It was permissible to write about farming because farming was still considered a noble and ennobling occupation; but it was not permissible, in the eyes of those who set the standards of literary taste, to write about factory workers, drummers, contractors, clerks, politicians, ward-heelers, canvassers, stenographers, actresses, lawyers, industrial buccaneers, and all the teeming life which made the clipping of coupons possible to those who decided, mainly women, what should or should not be written about.

Dreiser did begin to give us all this—the factory worker at work, the drummer on his trips, the ward-heeler in relation to his saloon and his henchmen, the industrialist in relation to his superintendents and these bosses in relation to their underlings. It was Dreiser's audacity in bringing this life, vivid and throbbing, into his pages that really shocked the prim schoolmasters and moral birchmen who sat in the chairs of criticism. They said that

Dreiser's novels were sexually corrupting and immoral; they attacked him on the score of indecency; they declared he wrote of "tom-cats" instead of men and gave a disproportionate and disgusting number of pages to the pursuit of the female by the male; they even accused him of blasphemy on the ground that swear words occasionally appeared in the mouths of his characters.

But, actually, whatever they pretended to be shocked at, they were actually shocked, not by Dreiser's frank treatment of the part the sexual relationship plays in life but by Dreiser's depiction of workers at work, of the process which made the publication of the old "cultural" magazines, the concerts, the operas and the art galleries possible. It was the "vulgarity" of Dreiser's novels which displeased them, not his reminding them that men and women have need of love.

In fact the manifestations of love, the mechanics of it, and the need for love occupy rather less space in Dreiser's novels than they do in life; for Dreiser is not a subtle psychologist like Stendhal, Proust or Lawrence, and is concerned more with the outward physical and psychical aspects of normal sexual attraction than with its aberrations. Dreiser's characters are comparatively simple and direct in their emotions. Hurstwood disintegrates under the force of an elementary grand passion for Carrie Meeber because Carrie, never swept away by love, is the stronger; Jennie Gerhardt is never quite awakened emotionally; Cowperwood needs women as a stimulant and an assurance, not as a fulfillment, for his fulfillment is in power—Cowperwood is more in love with intangibles than with women; the attraction Eugene Witla in *The "Genius"* has for women is the very thing which prevents him from ever fully realizing his potentialities in art—his emotional energy is sapped because he is not stronger than his own attraction: Clyde Griffith's love is the casual, egotistical love of the male adolescent. In *Twelve Men* Dreiser has given us twelve extraordinarily complete character studies without reference to women: in this book he is wholly concerned with the visions, the ideas, the work-motives of the men and he shows us how these visions, these ideas are expressed in the physical and mental activities of his subjects.

It is strange now for us to conceive of the difficulties Dreiser encountered in the first steps of his career as a novelist. Up until 1900, that is, up until his twenty-ninth year, Dreiser had never attempted to write fiction. After giving up newspaper work, wherein he had been an indifferent reporter, a good feature writer and (curious to reflect upon, considering the brooding somberness of his later work) a conductor of a column of humor, he earned a living as a free-lance writer for the magazines, contributing biographical studies of celebrities of the day—success stories of the "uplift" era. Associated with him at the time was another former newspaperman, Arthur Henry, who collaborated with Dreiser on many magazine articles and according to Vrest Orton (cf. *Dreiserana:*

New York, 1929) helped Dreiser to perfect his technique. Henry also persuaded Dreiser to try his hand at a short story, the while he engaged to write one himself. They sold both stories and with this success, Henry proposed that they should each try to write a novel. Dreiser sat down to a typewriter and typed out a title "Sister Carrie." That was as far as he got for a long time. Meanwhile Henry ground out in pain and self-doubt all but the concluding chapter of *A Princess in Arcady,* encouraged at every faltering step by Dreiser; then, weary and discouraged, he refused to go on with it. Dreiser, unwilling that so much labor should go for nothing, wrote the concluding chapter himself, whereupon the manuscript was dispatched to Doubleday, Page & Co., by whom it was duly published in 1900.

Dreiser, in his part of the agreement, was struggling with *Sister Carrie,* a novel that came slowly and laboriously, the characters taking on lineaments and personality and direction which he had not foreseen. He put the manuscript away several times and frequently said he could not go on with it; but Henry urged and encouraged him until the novel was finally completed in May, 1900. The novel was first submitted to Harper & Bros., and although Henry Mills Alden, then editor of *Harper's Magazine* found high merit in it, he was doubtful whether any American firm would have the courage to publish it. When Harper & Bros. turned it down, Alden suggested Doubleday, Page & Co., to Dreiser. At the time Frank Norris, already well

known as the author of *McTeague,* was a reader for
Doubleday, Page & Co., and by happy chance *Sister
Carrie* came to him first. He was rapturously enthusiastic
about it and communicated his enthusiasm to the owners
and editors, Frank Doubleday, Walter Hines Page, S. A.
Everitt, and Henry Lanier.[1]

A contract was drawn up; but meanwhile Mrs. Frank
Doubleday, who was engaged in moral reforms, read the
manuscript and was horrified. Her disapproval of the novel
was so active and violent that the firm notified Dreiser
that they had decided not to publish it. On Norris' advice,
Dreiser engaged a lawyer who forced them to carry out
the contract. Norris sent out 129 review copies to a select
list of critics and reviewers. No effort was made by the
sales department to bring the book to the attention of the
booksellers, although before the 423 copies of the first
edition of 1,008 copies were "remaindered," 465 were
sold.

The reception of *Sister Carrie* estopped Dreiser's
career as novelist for ten years, so violent and vindictive
was the moral indignation it stirred up. He suddenly found
all the editorial doors closed against him; former acquaintances cut him; and his source of income as a free-lance

[1] I derive this information on a mooted point from Vrest Orton's
valuable little book, *Dreiserana,* which is much more than a bibliography,
in that, among other things, it settles the question of the mythical Dreiser
book, listed in the 1899-1900 *Who's Who,* as *Studies of Contemporary
Celebrities,* a book contracted for but never published because of the
bankruptcy of the publishing firm that had commissioned it.

writer of articles was shut off, when it was noised about that he had written an "immoral" book.

At this time Dreiser was married and living in an apartment off Riverside Drive. He had married Sarah Osborne White, a teacher in a small backwoods town in Missouri, in 1898, after a romantic courtship lasting four years, which he has told about at length and candidly in *A Book About Myself*. Miss White was one of a group of school-teachers who had won a trip to the World's Fair in Chicago, in a popularity contest conducted by the St. Louis *Republic*. As a reporter on the newspaper, Dreiser was delegated to accompany the excursion and send back items of news. Dreiser fell in love with Miss White on the first day out from St. Louis. "She was in white," he writes, "with a mass of sunny red hair. Her eyes were almond-shaped, liquid and blue-gray. Her nose was straight and fine, her lips sweetly curved. She seemed bashful and retiring."

For two years he tried unsuccessfully to break down the reserves of this warm but strong principled young woman; but "In her was none of the variability that troubled me: if ever a person was fixed in conventional views it was she. One life, one love would have answered for her exactly. She could have accepted any condition, however painful or even degrading, provided she was bolstered up by the moral law." Her unapproachability only increased his ardor. He has described with humorous fidelity the costume he arrayed himself in to court her—

a costume he never dared to wear to the newspaper office where he worked, in consequence of which he often had to change clothing three times a day: "I indulged in a heavy military coat of the most disturbing length, a wide-brimmed Stetson hat, Southern style, gloves, a cane, soft-pleated shirts—a most *outré* equipment for all occasions including those on which I could call upon her or take her to a theater or restaurant." The gloves were bright yellow, he tells us, his shoes were narrow-toed patent leather; he wore a ring and a tie-pin and carried a cane.

Before he left for the East he became engaged to Miss White, with the customary assurances that he would send for her or come and claim her when he had got himself established in the world. And this, contrary to the usual fate of such assurances, he did—but not, as he saw it many years later when he wrote *A Book About Myself*, until "the first flare of love had thinned down to the pale flame of duty," and the edge of his devotion and desire had been dulled by experiences with other women. He regrets, in a poignant passage, that their love was not consummated the enchanting summer he visited her in her lovely village home: "There was about her an intense delight in living. No doubt she longed as much to be seized as I to seize her, and yet there was a moral elusiveness which added even more to the chase. I wished to take her then and not wait, but the prejudices of a most careful rearing frightened and deterred her. And yet I shall always feel that the impulse was better than the forces

which confuted and subsequently defeated it. For then was
the time to unite, not years later when, however much the
economic and social and religious conditions which were
supposed to surround and safeguard such unions had been
fulfilled, my zest for her, and no doubt hers in part for
me, had worn away."

That frustration and the subsequent imperfect com-
pensation for it in marriage, had much to do, I think, with
his later designation of himself as a "varietist" in love
and it may, too, have been in a measure responsible for
his militant, Nietzschean challenge to moral conventions.

But, nevertheless, this marriage in which duty had
become as much of a compelling force with him as romance, lasted all of twelve years before a separation took
place. And during those twelve years Mrs. Dreiser was
an industrious and economical housewife, who saw him
through the terrible and depressing years of ostracism and
poverty that followed the suppression of *Sister Carrie*.
He cracked under the strain of financial anxiety and self-
doubt; he and his wife went back to her parents' home;
he left her there after a time and returned to New York,
shabby, gaunt and discouraged. One day on Broadway
he encountered his jovial and Rabelaisian brother, Paul
Dresser (as Paul spelled his name), the comedian and
song-writer whom he describes so affectionately in *Twelve
Men*. Paul took him in hand, made him move into his
hotel with him and arranged to send him to William Muldoon's health sanitarium (Muldoon and his establishment

are described in *Twelve Men* under the title "Culhane the Solid Man").

After his experience at Muldoon's camp, he still felt he needed to get a grip on himself by outdoor labor and, through influence, he got a job with a construction gang on the New York Central railroad. He returned at length to the city, much restored in vigor and nerves, and presently he had put his writing career aside to become the editor of *Smith's Magazine,* a pulp-paper periodical supplying tales of adventure along the lines of *Pluck and Luck, Diamond Dick* and *Nick Carter.* He ran the circulation of Smith's up to 125,000, then switched to the *Broadway Magazine.* This was in the "muck-raking" era and Dreiser's editorial efforts were so successful in the direction that his salary went up to $100 a week while the circulation passed the hundred thousand mark. Thence he went over to the Butterick Publishing Co., as editor-in-chief of *The Delineator, The Designer, The New Idea,* and *The English Delineator,* at a salary that began at $7,000 and reached $25,000 a year before he resigned in 1910, fortified with savings which permitted him to resume his work of writing honestly and sincerely about life as he knows, and has experienced, it.

In 1910, encouraged by the enthusiastic reception of *Sister Carrie* in England while smarting under the treatment he had received in his own country, Dresier had begun *Jennie Gerhardt,* but put it aside and did not finish it until ten years later, a year after he had given up editorial work. It was published by Harper & Bros., who had turned down *Sister Carrie*. *Jennie Gerhardt* is a realistic Cinderella story containing some of his worst imagined scenes and some implausible dialogue, but it was somehow more acceptable to the puritanical taste of the reviewers and public than *Sister Carrie* in that Jennie was soft and appealing whereas Carrie Meeber was self-centered and ambitious, and Jennie's sin against the code ended in tragedy, *i.e.*, "punishment" for herself, whereas Carrie's sin ended in triumph for herself and tragedy for Hurstwood.

DREISER enjoyed fame and success for a fleeting while after *Jennie Gerhardt;* the book was greeted with praise in America as well as in England; Harper & Bros. gave him an advance on his next novel; and Grant Richards, an English publisher, arranged for him and Dreiser to make a tour in Europe for a series of impressions to be serialized in *Century Magazine* and later published in book form. The observations made on this trip are embodied in *A Traveler at Forty* (1913), a naïvely appealing book by a man hungry for beauty and consumed by curiosity.

With the publication of *The Financier* in 1912, Dreiser found himself a celebrity caught between puritans and antipuritans. H. L. Mencken, who had championed Dreiser from the first, saluted the book with enthusiastic reviews in the New York *Times* and in the *Smart Set*.

James Huneker, Edgar Lee Masters, and William Marion Reedy rallied around Dreiser, nominating him the foremost American novelist and the colossus to make a path through the thick forests of American prejudice and hypocrisy, but the schoolmarms in trousers and soprano-voiced reviewers set up the old battle cry of "immorality and indecency," and flung themselves on Dreiser tooth and nail.

Dreiser had drawn upon the career of Charles T. Yerkes, the buccaneering financier and traction magnate of Philadelphia and Chicago, for the first volume of a "trilogy of desire." It was the first picture (and still the best) of an energetic, powerful, acquisitive and sinister product of an era of greed and opportunity created by the rapid industrializing of the country under the influence of rapid transportation and the invention of labor-saving machinery. The second volume of the trilogy, *The Titan*, carried the career of Cowperwood through his adventures in Chicago, where, undeflected in his ruthless will to power by his defeat, disgrace and imprisonment in Philadelphia, he found more ample opportunities for his talent in the raw, new and mighty railroad center that Carl Sandburg has called "Hog-butcher to the World." *The Titan* called forth a new outburst of vituperation from the professional guardians of morals who closed their eyes to the reality everywhere manifested around them. As I write these words, Dreiser has not yet completed the trilogy. The third volume, which has been on the stocks for many years and frequently announced, is to show Cowperwood's further and final adventures when he went to London, armed with money, power and personality and set about achieving his ultimate ambition—to break into society. This novel should, if it follows its model, Yerkes, round out the drama as thoroughly as the third play in a trilogy by Sophocles or Euripides, because the *hubris* of Yerkes was humbled: there is nothing left of his fortune or of his schemes except one gesture toward things that endure— the Yerkes Observatory.

While still working on the last volume of the trilogy, Dreiser suddenly presented to an unsuspecting public, in two massive volumes, his first best seller, his first huge success—*An American Tragedy*.

Clyde Griffiths, the hero of *An American Tragedy*, is the least heroic of all the main characters in Dreiser's novels. It would seem that Dreiser had deliberately taken almost the least interesting and least sympathetic character he could imagine in the American scene in order to show his power to hold one's attention through two volumes each over 400 pages long. I say that it would seem so; but that is not Dreiser's method, not his purpose in life as he sees it, not his conception of the dignity of the novelist as a truth teller. It would seem also that he had chosen as a thesis a complete and devastating refutation of the frequently reiterated fallacy that the lack of religious training in the home is responsible for the waywardness and crimes of youth by giving a complete and compelling portrait and history of a boy who had the most pious and evangelical of parents and ended his life in the electric chair, convicted on a charge of murder. (Having been a reporter who has covered a number of murder trials, I can testify that I have not known one defendant who had not the benefit of religious training in the home, nor, indeed, a single one who did not become intensely sanctified just before going to the gallows.) But I am convinced that such a thesis was not in Dreiser's mind. His mind doesn't work that way. The famous Gillette murder case engaged his interest and set his mind upon the problem of unraveling the events in a boy's life that might lead up to the boy's death in the electric chair.

The result might be accepted as the great American novel if Dreiser had not already written at least two novels that may lay equal claim to such distinction— *Sister Carrie* and *The Financier*. As in those two novels, Dreiser has told a story in *An American Tragedy* that is peculiar to the American milieu. Murders happen in other countries, certainly, even murders of sweethearts by young men (though, to be accurate, Clyde did not actually commit the murder he premeditated but allowed the girl to drown in an accident without going to her aid); but all of the social forces leading up to the tragedy are special to the contemporary American scene.

To give one example: Clyde Griffiths plans the murder of a sweetheart of his own social and economic status in life when he realizes that her pregnancy means the shouldering of irksome responsibility and death to his hopes for financial and social advancement just at the moment when his hopes, after a hard struggle, seem about to be realized. In a land with a definite class system, like France, for instance, no such predicament would be possible. Even if it were imaginable that an uneducated French youth should rise from bellhop to the office management of a great industrial organization of which his uncle was the head, and that his social status was not prima facie settled by his relationship as nephew but was about to be established by his making good financially, he would need feel no moral or social concern about the girl if she were either in fact or potentially his social inferior. French custom tells the girl she must shift for herself; she was a mistress, without legal or social rights. Nor would a fiancée of the youth bother her head about his prenuptial indiscretions. The French mores are cruel. Dreiser says, "Look here, but so are the American mores in quite another way." And he shows us how.

The rise of Clyde Griffiths is common in American life. Throw a rubber ball into the crowd at Forty-second Street and Fifth Avenue and you would probably touch a dozen men before the ball stopped rolling whose intelligence, aspirations, education and careers up to the time Clyde began to plan the murder closely resemble those of Clyde.

One especially striking thing occurred to me after reading *An American Tragedy*. I call upon the newspaper reporters, lawyers, court functionaries and judges who may happen to read these lines to read the trial of Clyde Griffiths in Dreiser's novel and see if they do not bear me out in my statement that this is the first time that a murder trial has ever got into print—that is, the whole truth about a murder trial, the things which the reporters know and the lawyers know, but which cannot be part of a newspaper report. Such things, I mean, as how witnesses are coached, how evidence is rehearsed, how irrelevancies are emphasized and facts minimized for emotional effect upon the jury; above all, how in almost every sensational murder trial the real point at issue is not the conviction or freeing of the defendant but, on the side of the prosecuting attorneys, a bid for a political office, and—on the side of the attorney for the defense—a gamble for a reputation as a high-priced criminal lawyer.

Dreiser presents every aspect of such a trial with astounding dispassionateness from the moment the Coroner goes hotfoot with an incriminating bit of evidence to the District Attorney and discusses the case with him, not in terms of the guilt or innocence of the boy, but in terms of what the political advantages to them both will be if they work together and bring about a conviction. The bland self-interest of ordinary, respectable, good-natured human beings masking itself as interest in the public weal; the emotional issues that are whipped up in easily moved and gullible people, who want a victim when they can find one—all such facets of human character Dreiser depicts with masterly detail and authenticity. Each character involved in the trial stands out as thoroughly individualized, speaking entirely in character and in individual idiom, with his motives and prejudices, his convictions and his temperament understood and revealed through his words.

The story briefly is this: Clyde Griffiths is the son of an itinerant Methodist evangelist, who holds street-corner meetings and acts as a petty salesman from time to time to augment the meager family income. His mother is a stronger character than his ineffectual father, and she is patient in her endurance of their shabby lot; she bears her cross with true Christian fortitude, loves her brood and counsels her children to bear up under their adversities and have faith that the Lord will provide.

The Lord does not provide, and it is borne in upon Clyde's consciousness that the religious precepts of his father are worthless in the world of fact, when Clyde's sister runs away with a man who deserts her with child, and his mother is put to pitiable subterfuges to protect her daughter's name against the gibes of gossip and later to provide her with necessities she is unable to earn. Clyde achieves a measure of economic independence when he gets a job as bellhop in a leading hotel in Kansas City. He also is introduced to his first glimpse of luxury, of extravagance, of sexual phenomena and of vice.

Having long been the butt of the street urchins on account of his shabby clothes and his father's calling, he exults in his new ability to dress well, join the other bell-hops at drinking parties and spend money on girls. He gets a girl of his own, or thinks he has one, and she knows how to inveigle money out of him. Just as he had promised to buy the girl a fur coat his mother comes to him for money to help his sister out of urgent difficulties.

After a mild party at a roadhouse with his bellhop friends, one of them discovers that he must get the car back in a hurry to the garage before the owner, from whom it has been taken without permission, returns. The car runs over and kills a child; the situation becomes a thousand times more desperate to the youth at the wheel, and he speeds on, trying to elude the pursuers. Taking a side street, he rushes into a pile of building materials, wrecking the car and pinning himself and others, some unconscious, in the car.

Clyde crawls out, bleeding, and deserts the scene. Next he is heard of he is looking for a job in Chicago under an assumed name. He gets a job as bellhop in the Union League Club, where he encounters an uncle who is a prosperous business man in Lycurgus, New York, who offers him an opportunity to start at the bottom of his plant and make good if he can. He rises to the position of manager of a department in which there are twenty-five girls. With one of them he falls in love, and enters into a secret liaison.

He is a bright, good-looking, hard-working, promising chap and the younger people in the upper levels of Lycurgus society begin to take him up. He aspires to one of the girls in this society who flirts with him and falls in love with him. He wants to drop the other girl. At this point Dreiser writes the keynote: "So much for the effect of wealth, beauty, luxury, the peculiar social state to which he most aspired on a temperament that was as fluid as water."

But he cannot drop the other girl—it is too late. He seeks medical relief in an agonizing search. Then the notion, at first vague, comes to him to lure Roberta to a mountain resort on an intimation of marrying her, take her rowing upon a deserted lake, tip the boat and let her drown, at the same time leaving his hat floating on the water as if he (who would be using another name on the trip) were drowned also. He falters in his decision while they are on the lake, but an accident causes the boat to tip; the girl drowns without his attempting to aid her. He returns to his friends, tries to establish an alibi, but circumstantial evidence nets him, and he is tried, convicted of murder and sent to the chair, announcing that he has found Christ, that God has answered his prayers and that there is peace in his soul.

There you have the outline of a novel of such breadth, depth, and significance as only Dreiser could write. He is the most honest of all the realists I have ever read, not excluding Flaubert. Let others reiterate the stereotyped criticism that Dreiser writes badly because he uses such words as "chemism," "via" and "anent," lumbers along slowly when he is not narrating action or writing dialogue, but is merely about his ordained business of shirking no detail of his presentation of truth. Then let them read what every French critic and every eminent English critic of French literature, including Saintsbury (who translated Balzac) and Lytton Strachey has had to say about the style of Balzac. Finally let them read the pages describing the fatal automobile ride and the last chapter of the book and ask themselves if they know of any one who writes any better.

After *An American Tragedy* Dreiser began to take an active part in social and economic reform and published a heavily documented indictment of capitalism under the title, *Tragic America*. It is jumbled, impressive and angry, but his métier is to make the reader see and feel, not to lead a cause.

He has been the great incorruptible among American novelists in reflecting what he knows and has experienced and observed.

JAMES BRANCH CABELL

JAMES BRANCH CABELL

*

THE atmosphere and the background of the society into which James Branch Cabell was born and reared were vastly different from the atmosphere and background of the society into which Theodore Dreiser was born and reared. It is not surprising that the nature of their work, although contemporaneous and equally the subjects of early neglect, vilification and censorship, is so different, the one from the other, that superficially they might seem to have been the products of two different centuries in two different countries.

Dreiser was brought up in poverty in an industrialized North, in one of those dreary manufacturing towns where the ordinary hazards of the competitive struggle were intensified by the constant shifting of centers of market outlets and by booms and depressions. The society was heterogeneous and no stable culture had been developed. Cabell was brought up as a member of a vanishing aristocracy whose feudal traditions collapsed in the Civil

War and whose culture was disintegrating under the rising industrialization of the South. Dreiser received little formal education; Cabell taught Greek and French at William and Mary College after his graduation from that comparatively old institution.

Dreiser's life has been active and restless, Cabell's sedentary and contemplative. Dreiser's work has been moody and inquisitive, searching out motives as they are manifested in the actual lives of characters in his own peculiar time and place; Cabell's work has been (while quite as personal as Dreiser's) concerned with man's actual plight in all ages and times and with man's brave efforts to seem nobler in all respects than he is—a worthy effort which Cabell accepts with a smile of amusement behind which there is sadness mingled with hope and in which worthy effort he joins with a resolution to "write perfectly of beautiful happenings." (Cabell's conception of beauty is the poet's and the artist's conception and so embraces at times what the conventional-minded would term distasteful and the smutty-minded have called, on the statute books, "lewd, lascivious, indecent and obscene." Cabell's point may be explained, perhaps, by my saying that gluttony is an unpleasant act to contemplate but is beautiful when Rembrandt depicts it.

Literal-minded persons are sometimes astonished and disappointed when they learn that Cabell himself is a model of propriety, a respectable tax-paying citizen occupying a beautiful and formal brick house on Richmond-in-Virginia's wide avenue of trees and monuments to the equestrian heroes of the late War of the Confederacy; that he has been married but once and is quite ready to accept that once as his destiny; that he is a member of various learned societies, a historian and genealogist; and that he is a pew-holder and regular attendant at divine services of the Episcopal church, in whose tenets he believes quite as implicitly as he believes in anything that cannot be proved one way or the other.

These literal-minded persons seem to imagine, after reading his book (or at least those passages which somebody has told them are hot stuff), that he lives in a sort of Hollywood stage-set of the kind which is designed to suggest luxury and sin; that he is a practicing connoisseur of the most exotic forms of voluptuousness and ready at any moment to give demonstrations to any female who yearns for such instruction.[1] Thus they confuse the literary and imaginative artist with the madame of a brothel (who may, to be sure, occasionally be an artist in her own field but is more likely, even in her highest flights of iniquity, to be no more than an inept plagiarist from the Manual of Confessors which was compiled from some really fine flights of the imagination by libidinous eremites of the desert).

Despite a popular misconception, which arose over the public prosecution of *Jurgen* by the Society for the Suppression of Vice, Cabell is really interested in other

[1] *Special Delivery.*

matters that are subject to artistic treatment; and he bears a much closer resemblance to the author of the Gospel of Saint Mark, to Lucian, to Shakespeare, to Cervantes and to the Goethe of *Faust* than he does to the author of *The Memoirs of Fanny Hill*. (He has observed, in effect, however, that this is his monetary loss because most people are willing to attest to the general excellence of the classics, without reading them, and to go on reading things like *The Memoirs of Fanny Hill*.)

Cabell himself is at pains to make the point (which every reader who has read the eighteen volumes of *The Biography of Manuel* or any one of them should discover for himself) in his Author's Note to the Storisende edition of *Straws and Prayer-Books*:

"It is true enough, of course, that 'Domnei' exalts womanhood beyond our present-day, more prosaic beliefs, and that 'Jurgen' upholds the austere and strait-laced and temporarily unpopular doctrine that a married man had best remain faithful to his wife; just as it is likewise that 'Something About Eve' depicts a later Galahad who sets an example in the way of male chastity such as not many of our younger generation as yet under seventy-five are inclined to follow nowadays; and true also that 'The Silver Stallion' pleads frankly, with something it may be of the revivalist's blunt stridor, for the sustaining faith of old-fashioned religion. Yet these volumes touch upon many other matters; the spiritual message of these volumes is not wholly priggish; and, above all, the contents of any one volume may now fairly claim their right to be weighed in their just proportion to the whole eighteen volumes."

FEW of the more astute critics who have appraised the work of James Branch Cabell have failed to call attention to that extraordinary cohesion which marks the whole *Biography of Manuel* and his descendants. In the eighteen volumes which comprise the Storisende edition the scheme of each book seems to dovetail into the scheme of the other and the whole appears to be an uninterrupted discourse. The *Biography* didn't begin that way, you may be sure, but Cabell had the ingenuity, in revising his work, to give an illusion of continuity, not only by a subtly elaborate use of conjunctions, repetitions and reintroduction of characters from other books but also by setting his expertness in genealogy to the task of devising a family tree, in *The Lineage of Litchfield*, for the heroes and heroines he had imagined.

If this were an actual continuity, more tangible than that fluid abstraction we call the life force; if it were merely a tireless reiteration and recasting of characters, Mr. Cabell's work would have an unbearable monotony. But at bottom this apparent continuity has no more material existence than has the thread of lineal descent. To insist upon its importance is to obscure, as has been obscured, the epic range of Mr. Cabell's creative genius. It is to fail to observe that he has treated in his many books every mainspring of human action and that his themes have been the cardinal dreams and impulses which have in them heroic qualities. Each separate volume has a unity and harmony of a complete and separate life, for the excellent reason that with consummate skill he has depicted in each book one definite heroic impulse and its frustrations.

It is true, of course, that like the fruit of the tree of life, Mr. Cabell's artistic progeny sprang from a first conceptual germ—"In the beginning was the Word." That animating idea is the assumption that if life may be said to have an aim it must be an aim to terminate in success and splendor. It postulates the high, fine importance of excess, the choice or discovery of an overwhelming impulse in life and a conscientious dedication to its fullest realization. It is the quality and intensity of the dream only which raises men above the biological norm; and it is fidelity to the dream which differentiates the exceptional figure, the man of heroic stature, from the muddling, aimless mediocrities about him. What the dream is, matters not at all—it may be a dream of sainthood, kingship, love, art, asceticism or sensual pleasure—so long as it is fully expressed with all the resources of self. It is this sort of completion which Mr. Cabell has elected to depict in all his work: the complete sensualist in Demetrios, the complete phrasemaker in Felix Kennaston, the complete poet in Marlowe, the complete lover in Perion. In each he has shown that this complete self-expression is achieved at the expense of all other possible selves, and that herein lies the tragedy of the ideal. Perfection is a costly flower and is cultured only by an uncompromising, strict husbandry.

It is in humanity's records that it has reserved its honors for its romantic figures. It remembers its Cæsars, its saints, its sinners. It applauds, with a complete suspension of moral judgment, its heroines and its heroes who achieve the greatest self-realization. And from the splendid triumphs and tragic defeats of humanity's individual strivings have come our heritage of wisdom and of poetry.

Once we understand the fundamentals of Mr. Cabell's artistic aims, it is not easy to escape the fact that in *Figures of Earth* he undertook the staggering and almost unsuspected task of rewriting humanity's sacred books, just as in *Jurgen* he gave us a stupendous analogue of the ceaseless quest for beauty. For we must accept the truth that Mr. Cabell is not a novelist at all in the common acceptance of the term, but a historian of the human soul. His books are neither documentary nor representational; his characters are symbols of human desires and motives. By the not at all simple process of recording faithfully the projections of his rich and varied imagination, he has written eighteen books, which he accurately terms biography, wherein is the bitter-sweet truth about human life, and under the truncated name, Branch Cabell, has to date written a dozen books of commentary.

JAMES BRANCH CABELL was born in Richmond, Virginia, on April 14, 1879. His great-grandfather was William H.

Cabell, a governor of the state, and his maternal grand-father was Colonel James R. Branch of the army of the Confederacy. Five generations of Cabells had attended the College of William and Mary, and so, in due course, Cabell himself was graduated from there with a bachelor of arts degree. As an undergraduate he was an instructor in Greek and French and he, having won the chancellor scholarship (the highest scholastic honor), established a post-graduate course for himself in early French literature.

Shortly after his graduation, however, we find him working in the press-room of the Richmond *Times* and writing poems and short stories in his leisure in conscious imitation of Henry Harland, Justus Miles Forman, and Anthony Hope. He spent his twentieth and twenty-first years in New York as a reporter on the New York *Herald*. His job, it seems, was largely confined to reporting the society activities of Harlem, a district at that time not a sort of Ghetto for the Negroes but a high-toned residential section occupied by prosperous Dutch and German citizens. After two years in this work Cabell came to have such a phobia against New York City that it is with the greatest difficulty his wife can persuade him to go there even on the occasion of a marriage or a birth in his immediate family or of a literary festivity held in his particular honor.

In *Straws and Prayer-Books* we have a tender dialogue between the middle-aged Cabell and the twenty-two-year-old boy that he once was. The younger Cabell is asking the elder Cabell whether he would advise him "to become a regular writer," now that he has written five short stories and mailed them all out together and has had three of them accepted and has got one hundred and five dollars for the lot of them. ("Mr. Alden wrote me a nice letter about the one I sent to *Harper's* and said they would be very glad to use it if I would let them say 'paunch' where I had written 'belly.' ")

". . . I would like to write the very nicest sort of books,—like Henry Harland's, and Justus Miles Forman's, and Anthony Hope's. They would be about beautiful fine girls and really splendid young men, and everything would come out all right in the end, so they could get married, and not be sort of bitter and smart-alecky and depress people"—he coughed—"the way some people do."

This young Cabell is fat, "remarkably fat for a lad of twenty-two or thereabouts; and he had, as I noticed first of all, most enviably thick hair, sleeked down, and parted 'on the side,' with some fanfaronade in the way of capillary flourishes. He was rather curiously dressed, too, I considered: the lapels of his coat were so abrupt and small and stiff that they must be held in place, I deduced, by a coat-spring, which would be today, I could have no doubt, the only coat-spring in existence. Then, too, he wore a fawn-colored waistcoat, and his rigorous collar towered, incredible in height, above a sky-blue 'Ascot tie,' which was resplendently secured with a largish sword-hilt asparkle everywhere with diamonds. And to describe the majestic rotundities of this boy's shoulders as due to 'padding' would be, through understatement, to deceive you; since these coat-shoulders could have been designed and builded (I reflected), by no imaginable tailor, but only by an upholsterer."

Thus began a literary career, initially successful with short stories accepted here and there and with the publication of *The Eagle's Shadow* as a serial in *The Saturday Evening Post*. On Cabell's return to Richmond from New York he worked as a reporter on the Richmond *News* for one year and thereafter, according to *Who's Who*, "conducted genealogical and original research work in America, France, Ireland and England." The fruits of these genealogical pursuits are to be found in the privately printed books, *Branch of Abington, Branchiana*, and *The Majors and Their Marriages*. In them are the first indices of the irony that was to characterize his later work. He who would write pretty love stories in which everything came out all right in the end discovered very early, in his examination of the records of his ancestors, that this happy consummation was not, to understate the matter, inevitable.

THIS literary career, thus romantically begun, he has pursued through some thirty-odd years with an uncompromising fidelity to his chosen rôle as an artist of letters. He writes, he tells us, for, and in a special sense, his own diversion. This literary career has been attended by many

vicissitudes: he wrote and published books for some four-
teen years without any special recognition and it was not
until *Jurgen* was inadvertently advertised by the Society
for the Suppression of Vice that he achieved any considerable monetary reward or reached best-sellerdom.

That wise and witty book I consider to be among the
world's masterpieces of imaginative literature, although
The High Place and *The Silver Stallion* rank with it. In a
private letter to me, Cabell has given me the "genesis" of
that "Comedy of Justice," which I append for its historical
importance, its revelation of how a masterpiece came to be
written, and for the insight it gives into the part played by
the subconscious in a great work of the imagination.

".. . It was a year ago last March that I temporarily
put aside my Something about Eve to write for Mencken
the short story he requested and seemed to merit. I evolved
then very much the same Some Ladies and Jurgen in imagination as eventually appeared in The Smart Set:
wherein the devil offers Jurgen the three symbolic ladies
Guenevire and Cleopatra and Helen, and the poet prefers,
upon the whole, his prosaic wife. But as I wrote it out, I
scented possibilities—how much more effective, for instance, it would be if Jurgen had previously known and
loved and lost these women. Of course, that meant, to me,
a dizain, with four tales already suggested: it would be
out of space and time, of necessity, if Jurgen were to encounter these three who lived centuries apart. So, with

my story still unwritten, I began to plan the dizain, of ten short stories to be disposed of severally for much fine gold. Ah, but the Cleopatra episode! here I foresee myself heading straight for an imitation of *Aphrodite* and Louys' notion of life in Alexandria. Well, then, let us substitute the goddess herself in place of the Cleopatra who symbolizes her, and call the goddess—no, not Aphrodite, the Grecianisms must be reserved for the Helen part. I consider her other names, and am instantly captivated by the umlaut in Anaïtis. So my second heroine becomes Anaïtis, a moon goddess. But her lovers are solar legends. . . . Why, to be sure, for does not Guenevire typify the spring, Anaïtis summer, and Helen in her Leuhe avatar the autumn? I perceive that Jurgen is a solar legend, and inevitably spends the winter underground. There is the Hell episode postulated, then. So I make out my calendar, and find it 37 days short, since obviously the year must be rounded out. Where was Jurgen between 22 March and 30 April? The question answers itself, and I spy the chance to use that fine idea that has been in my mind for fifteen years or more, as to how Heaven was created.

"I am getting on now, with my dizain lacking only three episodes—since the half-written magazine story has obviously split into an opening and an ending of a book. (That is, I thus far think it the ending.) And now I am wondering if there is not a chance at last for that other fine idea I could not ever find a place to work into—the going back to a definite moment in one's past . . . For

what? . . . obviously for a woman, since Jurgen has by this
time taken form as a person. . . . What woman, though?—
why, clearly the woman who in his youth represented the
never quite attainable Helen. And she was Count Em-
merick's second sister, whose existence I had postulated in
The Jest, with the intention of using her in due time. I
christen her Varvara, in general consonance with my Russian Koshchei, who I am beginning to perceive must be
more than a mere devil if the book is to ascend. . . . Yes,
he must be the Demiurge, and God his creation. . . . Then
Koshchei must be rather stupid, and not be bothering himself about Jurgen at all. I need another supernatural agent,
some one more near to purely human affairs, to direct
Jurgen's wanderings. My mind being already on Russian
mythology, and the regaining of a lost day being involved,
the Leshy who control the days present themselves, and I
select Sereda for Jurgen to wheedle out of, of course, one
of the Wednesdays when he was young. Another episode.

"But this Varvara (no, nobody will be certain as to
the pronunciation of Varvara: call her Dorothy)—will dis-
appoint him, a little anyhow, if he goes back to the actual
girl. Really to go back, he must return to the girl as she
seemed to him, and himself be young again. . . . But the
point is already in my mind that, while Jurgen is to keep
the youth that would come back to him with the replevined
Wednesday, so far as his body goes, his mind is to remain
middle-aged. So I grope to the ironic scheme of letting
him win to his ideal girl as he actually is, and be to her

unrecognizable. . . . Then he must, somehow, get rid of his false youth before his interview with Koshchei in the cave: that makes me the tenth episode. . . . No, I still lack the machinery for getting him to the Garden: a Centaur appears the handiest method of combining transportation and conversation. I think inevitably of Nessus, then of his shirt. Yes, something must be done with that shirt. . . . And that episode must come first, while Jurgen is still middle-aged.

"Well, there you are. That is about how the outline of the book came to me: and at this stage I went back to the Smart Set story and actually wrote it. Thereafter I set about writing my ten episodes (and found them resolutely determined not to be short stories, on any terms); and rewrote them; and put in here and there just anything which occurred to me, and changed this and altered that; and groped to that loathsome last chapter as the tale's inevitable ending. And almost last of all, I pivoted the whole thing upon the shadow and the shirt, which were almost the last things of all I thought of. . . . So, you see, the book virtually wrote itself."

WHEN Cabell reached his fiftieth year he announced the conclusion of *The Biography of Manuel* the Redeemer by saying that at fifty a writer's creative years were on the wane and that hence there would be no more literary work from the pen of James Branch Cabell. But a writer writes as long as he has breath in his body, for writing is his reason for existence and in the highest sense his pleasure. So, although James Branch Cabell ceased to exist, Branch Cabell came upon the scene in 1929 with a regularity of production that is the ear-mark of the confirmed artist in letters, and began to produce commentaries on his own work and on the contemporary scene which betray no lessening of his powers for acute observation, irony, wit, satire and loveliness of phrase.

Cabell's ultimate conclusion about life? His answer: "My protagonist sides, in brief, with Rabelais and with Montaigne and with Socrates: and at the last can but echo, more or less variously, the *Peutetre* and the *Que sais-je?* and the more frank 'I don't know' of these contented sceptics."

INDEX

*

Stoics, the, 164-165
Strachey, Lytton, 269
Suetonius, 64, 65 *n.*, 70, 95 *n.*, 143;
    Lives of the Twelve Cæsars,
    115
Summers, Montague, *History of
    Witchcraft and Demonology*,
    186 *n.*
Swift, Jonathan, 156

Tacitus, 63, 70, 91, 94, 96, 97;
    the *Annals*, 92-93, 115, 143
Tailhade, Laurent, translation of
    The Satyricon of Petronius
    into French, 114
Talmud, the, 49
Tarpeian Rock, Rome, 56, 78
Terence, 119
Thomas, the apocryphal gospel of,
    30
Thucidides, 160, 166
Tiberius, the Emperor, 88
Tigellinus, 92, 93
Times, the New York, 260
Timocles the Stoic, 123 *ff.*
Timothy, 33
Titans of Literature, 9
Titian, 193, 194
Titus, the Emperor, 31, 42, 56, 77,
    79, 94, 95 *n.*
Trajan, the Emperor, 137 *n.*
Trotsky, 210
Tyndall, 249

Vasari, 201
Verus, Lucius, 140-143
Vespasian, the Emperor, 63-64 and
    n., 79
Virgil, 190
Virgin birth of Christ, the, 25-26,
    34, 53
Vitellius, the Emperor, 141
Voltaire, 121, 156

Wagner, 212, 215
Washington, George, 26
Whibley, Charles, 119-120, 132,
    176, 182; *Studies in Frank-
    ness,* 115, 180-181, 206
Wilde, Oscar, translation of *The
    Satyricon* of Petronius attrib-
    uted to, 113-114
William and Mary College, 274,
    280
Wodehouse, P. G., 120
Wright, Wilmer Cave, 170

Xenophon, 143

Yerkes, Charles T., 261
Yerkes Observatory, the, 262

Zangara, Giuseppe, would-be assas-
    sin of President Franklin D.
    Roosevelt, 22
Zeus, 7, 123 *ff.*
Zimmern, Helen, 215